The Spirit Gives Life

HOW I LEARNED TO MEDITATE

Malcolm Smith

TWS | THE WRITER'S SOCIETY PUBLISHING

Copyright © 2023 by Malcolm Smith

All rights reserved.

No part of this book may be reproduced in any form or by any electronic or mechanical means, including information storage and retrieval systems, without written permission from the author, except for the use of brief quotations in a book review.

To request permissions, contact TWS Publishing at www.thewriterssociety.online

Paperback: ISBN 978-1-961180-23-9

>TWS | The Writer's Society Publishing
>Lodi, CA
>www.thewriterssociety.online

Contents

Prologue	1
Chapter 1	5
Chapter 2	9
Chapter 3	17
Chapter 4	23
Chapter 5	35
Chapter 6	43
Chapter 7	51
Chapter 8	61
Chapter 9	69
Chapter 10	79
Chapter 11	89
Chapter 12	101
Chapter 13	117
Chapter 14	125
Chapter 15	135
Chapter 16	145
Chapter 17	153
Chapter 18	163
Chapter 19	173
Epilogue	181
About the Author	183
Also by Malcolm Smith	185
Publisher Information	187

Prologue

The most powerful meditation practiced on earth is that which is a result of the faith that centers upon Jesus Christ the Lord.

When the average Westerner thinks of a Christian meditating, he usually pictures a monk or a nun in a cloister or a cell. Meditation is looked upon as the activity of an elite few, certainly not the experience of the corporate business executive or a busy housewife.

In its inception, Christianity was the most secular of all world religions. It was an invasion by the Holy Spirit into the world of industry, big business, classroom, and family life. It was not a dead philosophy — Jesus was alive from the dead and Lord of all. People from every level of society entered into a mystical union with Him and became Christian meditators. Their secular lives were transformed into a Holy of Holies.

Jesus was no hermit, a fact that the professional holy men of His day delighted to throw in His face. Jesus enjoyed eating and drinking and all types and conditions of men, and He was called '…a gluttonous man and a drunkard, a friend of tax-gatherers and sinners!... .' (Matthew 11:19)

Jesus quietly walked with His Father in the dust and shavings of a carpenter's shop for ninety percent of His life. His meditation was in the midst of hammer blows and the rasping of a saw. His audience was peasant folk with big, rough hands and weather-beaten faces. Paul described the first Christians in 1 Corinthians 1:26, "…there were not many wise according to the flesh, not many mighty, not many noble." These kinds of people were the first to enter the dynamic path of meditation, and within a few years, their practice had turned the Roman Empire upside down.

These very ordinary people who meditated under the Lordship of Jesus walked through life radiating peace with singing hearts. They were in union with the infinite, personal God. As they meditated, they consciously drew upon His wisdom, love, and power. They were able to transcend the pressures of the environment. They were in accord within themselves, walked in peace with their fellow man and in harmony with their universe.

Over the last two decades, there has been a renewal of Spirit-led Christianity throughout the Church. Thousands of ordinary Christians are realizing that meditation, as taught in the Scripture, is the responsibility and privilege of every disciple of Jesus the Lord.

Prologue

The meditator encounters the living God, entering into vital communication and fellowship with Him. God is not the cosmic Impersonal, but the living, personal God who calls men to listen to Him and be listened to. The Bible is impregnated with this sense of the aliveness of God.

To anyone who will stop and listen, He immediately brings them into His fellowship. Christianity is the religion of knowing God through Jesus the Lord and coming into harmony with Him through meditation.

In the following pages, I share how I became a Christian meditator. There was no one to teach me, and I learned slowly and, sometimes, painfully. It is my personal story, culled from old notebooks and journals, vivid memories of spiritual milestones that are as real today as if they had happened last night.

Anyone who tries to relive my experience will defeat my purpose and waste their own time. It is the *principles* I discovered that are for everyone. They are open secrets to be adopted and used by everyone with ears to hear.

Chapter 1

My first memory of life was some time at the end of my first year, a few weeks before my second birthday, October 1940. I was asleep, but I vividly remember the floral wallpaper I was awakened to as someone reached into my high-sided cot and scooped me from my blankets. They ran, holding me to the stairs that ran steeply down to the living quarters. The garish wallpaper continued down the stairs, and as I was jolted and swayed in the person's arms, the wallpaper was a few inches from my face.

We reached the last stair and came to a smaller door that seemed to open under the stairs. I was thrown in, landing on a pile of blankets, followed by the person who had carried me thus far, who landed on top of me. A booming sound shattered the silence somewhere far away, and the body on top of me pressed me into the blankets.

Years later, I discovered this to be the beginning of the Blitz – Hitler's plan at the beginning of WW2 to reduce London to a pile of ashes by the continual bombing of the city for 57 consecutive days and nights. I entered the world of terror, but for me, I did not know the name of the fear, nor its when and why. I learned the fear by the wail of the air raid siren that announced the run to the shelter and being squashed into some tiny space with no windows, watching adults hold their breath while the sound of explosions a few miles away rocked our house.

A short while after that first experience, men came to the house with steel sheets and constructed a steel room inside our living room. That room would become the focus of our life. We ate from its top; it was an exciting play place for my two cousins who lived in the house with their mothers and me. But every night, many times during the daytime, the terrifying sound of the air raid siren cut into our world and urgently summoned everyone from the bedroom, kitchen, and garden to run to the little door that led to the room under the steel table. We would huddle there, listening to distant booms and explosions.

We lived in North London in a suburb called St. Albans, which had been the Roman Military camp serving Roman London or Londinium as it was then known. We were in danger of Hitler's bombs, but the direct hits were in central London and especially the London Docks with its ships from all over the world.

My father was in the fire department. The Nazi bombs were accompanied by incendiary bombs that set everything on fire as they exploded. The fire department followed the bombs to put out the fire that was guaranteed to be burning as the chaos of the bombing had quietened down.

Chapter 1

He would be gone for weeks at a time to the cities and towns all around the coast of England that were the target of the deadly bombs. He then came home for a week of rest. He seemed to know where the focus of the bombing would be on some nights. He had been injured and was back home on sick leave. The siren announcing another night of bombing had summoned us all awake and heading for the shelter. My father said as the siren wound down its wail, "They are not coming here tonight!" he assured me, and then, "I want to show you something you will never forget!" We walked the hill to the top of our road, and as we crested it, London lay spread below us. I watched in horror as bombs exploded across the horizon, the RAF planes were firing at the German aircraft, and I watched the crippled planes spiral down in a ball of fire. Fire from the bombs had sprung up across London until the city seemed to be a cauldron of one great fire. The evening wind brought the acrid smell of exploded bombs, giving me the feeling that I was not viewing from a distance but engulfed in the battle. Between the explosions, the bells rang furiously from the center of the smoke and flames as ambulances and fire trucks demanded clear passage, edging their way in and out of the flames and the death that reigned from the sky.

"This is Hitler's big night, but he will never win! There will always be an England!" My father was a quiet man, but that night, his eyes shone, his voice louder than I had heard before, and a triumph that translated to my young heart.

Some may think my father was terrorizing me, even abusing me, taking me to that hilltop to witness the battle that raged a few miles away across the center of London and somewhat below us, giving us front-row seats to this macabre scene.

Until that night, I did not understand the fear that sat on every adult's face, a fear without a name, not discussed when children were around – but a nameless fear that settled into my soul, tormenting me. Kindergarten treated it all as a game: who could be the first to put on the Mickey Mouse gas mask straight, and who would get into the bomb shelter before the others in our endless practice drills?

On that fateful night, I realized it was no mere game. As I looked into the monstrous mouth of death and hell, I understood fear had a face. The piercing wails of sirens served as an urgent warning, compelling us to seek refuge beneath the shelter of the steel table in our living room, all in a desperate attempt to escape the clutches of this monstrous, looming death.

The war dragged on, and my birthdays were with it. We sat around the steel table every Christmas and listened to the King's speech. He had a terrible stutter, making it difficult to understand. At other times, we sat around the radio and listened to Big Ben toll and call for the nation to listen, and Winston Churchill would speak in a raspy voice I can remember to this day. I didn't understand, but the seriousness leaped from the adults, churning my little boy emotions into the white caps that the gale winds left in their wake on the river Thames.

Chapter 2

I lay on the tartan blanket bunched up in the bomb shelter. My gran was talking, filling the silence as we waited for the all-clear siren to scream its message. She had just announced the war would soon be over, Hitler was losing, and his generals wanted to surrender. She had a plan to have us move house. I remember her tired old voice rising with authority.

She explained how the German bombers followed the River Thames from the English Channel right into the center of London, where they dropped their load of death and then headed back down the River Thames to Germany. In the pre-war days of peace, the path they followed was the tourist paradise, for the crowds that poured out of London in the summer months to fill the beaches that skirted the Thames River, the hundreds of kiosks selling shellfish and to buy the trinkets that announced they had been to Southend. Up behind were small hotels and boarding houses filled with tourists who could afford a week at the beach.

But in these days of war, the German bombers flew back to home base across all of the hotels, B and B, and larger boarding houses and, wanting to be home fast, threw out all the extra cargo, unused bombs, and incendiary bombs as they flew over the hotels.

There was the possibility of a German land invasion, and that entire area of the beaches would then have become the front line of defense. It was enclosed with barbed wire, and every few yards, a cement box served as a gun turret that could sweep the beach with bullets.

It was the front line of defense, potentially very dangerous, in line for a nightly discarding of unused bombs, and my gran's idea was that we should buy a hotel there and wait out the end of the war! "Hotels are being given away," she said excitedly, "Hitler is ready to surrender, and once the war is over, all of London will be wanting a holiday by the sea. Buy now, and we will be ready to fill our hotel!" I fell asleep on the floor. All I knew in my overhearing conversations was that we had no money and were described as "dirt poor."

I heard no more, but in a short while, a moving van carried everything we owned to the beach and hotels on the other side of London. We were poor, and before I was born, they had come through the depression and then plunged into the war.

Before the war, where we were moving to was considered a semi-rich area; we moved in a run-down truck into the path of Nazi bombs and purchased a hotel that, in better days, we could not afford to stay in, let alone buy.

Chapter 2

My gran was right! The war ended with dancing in the streets and fireworks filling the sky. There were few civilians, but they made a noise that matched the fireworks. No one told me what was going on, and with explosions outside my bedroom window, I hid under the bed!

People quickly moved back into their homes, and others bought hotels and fine houses.

Our next-door neighbors looked horrified as my cousins and I played in the street on a Sunday. They bundled us up and took us to their church —a Bible church that preached the Gospel — a Gospel I had never heard before.

It was not long before I was repeating a prayer to accept Jesus after my Sunday school teacher. I came home, and hardly knowing the meaning of the words I used, I told my mother that I had "got saved."

My mother had a very religious background in what amounted to a cult. Apparently, in her teens, she had stood in the Sunday morning service where speaking was for men only and announced that she wanted to smoke, drink, dance, and have a man! The entire family was excommunicated, and when I was born, there was no mention of the Gospel, Bible, or Jesus. But when I told my mother of my Sunday school prayer, she knew what I was trying to say.

At that same time, my mother was invited to an Elim Pentecostal Church – very much the same as the Assemblies of God in the US.

We ended up going to a Sunday evening service, which was geared to visitors and the unsaved. We had hardly sat down before someone began speaking loudly in a foreign language. My mother looked at me and whispered loudly, "We're getting out of here!"

The person speaking stopped, and before we could flee the building, the pastor began to speak in English — I did not know my mother's story, but I discovered later that without mentioning her name, he told her life story, finishing with a call to come back to Him – not to the cult!

We had been introduced at the deep end to the Holy Spirit's gift of tongues and interpretation. My mother had lost it during the pastor's interpretation and sobbed uncontrollably. I did not know what was going on and was embarrassed.

We began attending the Elim church, and in a few weeks, my mother had an experience of the Holy Spirit in the early morning hours. She was in the kitchen speaking in a foreign language, but with such joy, it reverberated through the house. I hid under the pillow.

I wanted out of this church with its loud (joyous) singing, physical welcome to the church given at the door in hugs (in England!?), and the strange happenings when one was said to receive the Spirit. I went to the youth group at the church our neighbors had taken me to and settled into their quiet meetings where I could be unnoticed.

Chapter 2

The formative years in the war had left a deep mark on me; looking back, it was a type of PTSD. I was afraid of people that would be friends and intrude into my life – I was afraid of life! I found it difficult to talk to anyone and preferred being alone, avoiding contact with people. The Bible church fitted well where I was almost invisible. I ignored their messages on the need to witness to friends. I had no friends and did not talk to anyone about such intimate things as what they believed about Jesus.

Then, one of the youth group, Colin, asked me to go with him to a church where he could be prayed for — he was sick and heading for surgery, so he needed divine healing. He had found such a church and wanted me to go with him for moral support. The church was the Elim church in an outlying country district. I groaned inside but mustered courage and agreed to go with him.

Ashingdon was a small country town, and the church was a one-room corrugated iron shed; a prayer room was through a door on the platform. I stood at the back, looking for a rapid exit.

As the preacher from the US spoke — he tended to shout more than talk — I felt a kind, gentle presence, an awakening to an accepting love at the center of my being. I felt delighted in! Joy seemed to take over every cell in my body. A feeling akin to sweet oil being poured over me, beginning with my head and gently, slowly over my shoulders. I wanted to run fast and far! I had a fleeting thought – this must be what had happened to my mother at three in the morning. But the love and acceptance, the peace (the first time in my life), the joy that welled in me, eager to express, was too good to run from. I stood torn between staying and letting this feeling finish what had begun or run and never return. I uneasily chose to stay and let the presence engulf me.

I had not been aware of what the American pastor was preaching about, but suddenly realized he had finished speaking and began to call people to walk forward to make a decision for Christ. I was relieved; maybe I could slip away and let what was happening finish out on the road away from all the people. Instead, I heard him say, "Those who want to receive the Spirit come to the prayer room…" I found myself running down the aisle, dodging the people who had come to the front for whatever reason. I went up the steps to the platform two at a time and almost fell through the door into the adjacent prayer room. No one was there, just benches at which to kneel and pray. No one came in. I was alone in the Presence of the Spirit. The strange language I had heard my mother use at 3 in the morning was in my head as belonging to me. Strange words arose in my speech center, and I began to speak them, which released a river of joy and love that cascaded through my body and soul, sweeping all fears before it.

I came out at 2:30 in the morning. The pastor was waiting to lock up. He had chosen to leave me alone in my awakening to the Spirit, for which I am eternally grateful in case some might think I was "taught" how to act and speak. He had never met me before. I was 13, coming on 14, and had never spoken or done anything publicly. He said, "God met with you tonight son!" I enthusiastically agreed. Then, "I want you to come on Sunday night and tell the congregation what happened to you tonight." I felt a strange joy at the offered opportunity and said, "I'll be here!"

Colin had been healed and was full of joy, and the two of us cycled into the misty darkness, sharing our experiences with each other. It was Tuesday in early February 1952; the night frost was showing on the roadside bushes, and our breath was like steam in the air as we pedaled our bicycles through the countryside.

Suddenly, it dawned on me that I was committed to speaking to a congregation in five days. An old fear rose in my gut, and for a moment, I thought I would throw up, but with it, another inner Voice that carried authority assured me all was and would be well.

I do not know what I said that Sunday, but I knew it was the beginning of something I had never dreamed of!

At the time of writing this chapter, that Sunday is coming on 72 years ago! I have preached almost every Sunday since that day and have taught the Scripture on every continent.

That night of awakening to the Person of the Spirit is the only explanation for my life.

Chapter 3

In the days that followed, I was adjusting my life to the Person who had moved in and was quietly taking over. The sense of being loved in a way I had never known before; the swelling of joy and peace did not leave but became the canvas on which my life was being painted. Above all, Jesus became real to me as never before. It seemed that the Spirit was silently pointing out who He was and what He had done — it was attended by a longing to know more of Him.

What followed did not happen either all at once or in complete clarity and understanding. I am writing this chapter over 70 years from when this book you are about to read took place, and it has taken all of that time to come to know the Person of the Spirit, yet in so saying, when each insight was given, it never felt lacking but fully satisfied me at that time.

The first of such insights put me at odds with the vocabulary of the people in the church. When they spoke of their encounter with the Spirit, they spoke impersonally; they described the event and the feelings, but little was said of the Spirit being the Person who is realized to fill one's life and to have been in and with us through the years we never even knew that He existed!

I had returned to the Elim church after the meeting with the Spirit, and in the youth group, I was bombarded with questions that reflected what I had heard the church speak of as their experience of the Spirit.

"So, you got the baptism? What's it like?"

"Did you seek it for a long time?" "What happened when it came?" "Are you filled with it all the time?"

A visiting pastor; "I seek the anointing; I cannot speak without it!"

"When were you filled with the baptism?"

I am not saying any of these phrases reflect what the Elim church believed, but this is what church members and the youth group leadership said to me in those early days.

No doubt I had an experience, and they were trying to put a name to the experience that had some relationship to the Scripture. I gathered my experience was called "the baptism with the Spirit," "being filled with the Spirit," and when you felt the Presence, you were said to have the "anointing." But I did not hear anyone speak of the Spirit as Person, only in terms of His impersonal effects. It bothered me because my first attempt to explain was in terms of the Person moving in to share my life who was attended by many effects!

With the settling in to describe His Presence in terms of the effects, it became apparent that it was expected that those who were baptized in the Spirit had to work at maintaining the feelings of the effects of that moment. Special revival meetings kept the expectancy high as everyone was expected to go to the prayer room and duplicate what happened when they "received."

I realized that the Scripture spoke of the Spirit as Person in the same language as Jesus was Person, except the Spirit was invisible, and His original voice was inaudible but very real. He is described as the center of joy, even laughter and dancing; He can be grieved and told to be quiet. He was in attendance at the leadership meetings of the church and made His mind plain to them and endorsed their decisions. He spoke in people, directed their plans, and made those plans known to the leadership. He gave insight, clarity of mind, and the ability to communicate to those who announced the Gospel. He communicated the power of the resurrection to live the life of Jesus. Above all, He made Jesus real and opened inner eyes to see His magnificence. He enabled believers to share their faith in their lives and words.

It became increasingly plain to me that He is not an impersonal 'it' that is associated with the effects of His Presence but the Person who becomes our closest and dearest Friend who lives in us – in our bodies – and shares with us all that God the Father and the Son would say to us.

He is not merely a Person but the Person of God here with us and in us today. He shares in the Trinity and is co-equal to the Father and the Son, God with and in us.

He does not come and go! He has been with us since before we were born, and now that we have awakened to Him, He delights in true relationship and fellowship with us. He never leaves us. He is the gift of God to us and was not given because we were good enough, nor because we wanted Him enough — but because He wanted to be in us, sharing our life forever.

He has a specific work to do sharing our life. He is the Teacher, the Guide leading us into all Truth (Jesus is the Truth). The original language suggests "taking us by the hand and leading us into hitherto unknown territory, into all truth." He uncovers what we would otherwise not see and opens our eyes that have been blinded by Satan and by religion that has closed eyes to much that belongs to the believer.

Over months and years, I learned to be aware of the Spirit — the Person of shimmering light, brimming with joy, the source of peace. Every time I read the Scripture, sat meditating, or was about my everyday business, I paused to be aware He was with me, in me, ready to light up Scripture, and to give understanding and wisdom in every circumstance. He communicates to us the ascended life of Christ and makes Galatians 2:20 a reality wherever we are.

As you read the following pages, understand that this adventure of knowing the Spirit was going on the entire time I learned to meditate. To begin with, I did not know He was my Mentor from the beginning. He called me on the beach; He led me to the paraphrase of the New Testament epistles. He drew me to the old gate of the churchyard and had me sit there and learn to meditate. He made me see the dog, Banjo, running after butterflies and the sheep and cows chewing the cud, enlightening me to realize what it all meant.

He opened my eyes to the glory of Jesus and taught me how to teach the multitudes around the world. He gives the compassion that reaches to lay hands on the sick and speak what He gives into the broken heart.

Without the Spirit, I would be sitting in the back row of a church, running out before anyone could talk to me. I would live in a state of fearing people and all of life. But the goal of Jesus shedding His blood and resurrection from the dead is to give us His Spirit, and I am today who I am because of His gift that I received in a corrugated shed 71 plus years ago.

Chapter 4

Beginnings are very hard to trace. A thought that seems to stray into our minds like a lost puppy may actually be a nudge from God's Spirit. A cry that rises from deep within and finds articulation in our minds can be the beginning of a path that will take a lifetime to follow.

As I made my way to the beach on a grey November Saturday in 1953, I did not dream that I was starting out on a new dimension of the Christian life.

The fog had rolled in the night before. I had lain awake listening to the moan of fog horns that punctuated the minutes with monotonous regularity from the ships moored in the estuary of the river Thames a few hundred yards from our home.

That day, Saturday, I had escaped to the beach wrapped in its grey blanket, the rocks and stones strewn with black, dried-out seaweed tossed there by last week's violent storm. But, this morning, the river's edge was a cocoon of silence, my footprints the only disturbance in the sand. Overhead, the melancholy cry of a seagull joined the lapping of the waves at my feet, the only other sound to join with the ships' horns. Behind me was Thorpe Bay, and somewhere up ahead was Southend Pier, the longest in the world, stretching over a mile into the estuary.

I became aware that my hair, covered in minuscule water droplets, was clinging to my forehead. I drew my coat around me. It wasn't cold, but the damp, chill air made me shiver. I breathed deeply, savoring the tangy odor of seaweed and tar mixed with every type of shellfish.

The beach narrowed, and I knew I was approaching the pier. Amusement arcades and gift shops crowded the beach a hundred yards to my right. Each summer and early fall, thousands of visitors from London thronged the beaches and sidewalks, buying trinkets labeled "A Gift from Southend" while eating from tiny plates piled high with raw shellfish harvested daily from the miles of riverbed exposed by the outgoing tide. This morning, all was silent, the gift shops boarded up, and the stalls covered over, all at rest in the clinging mist. Rowboats, upside down on the stones anchored to the sidewalk, lay neatly along the beach. I slumped down on one of them, surveying what I could see on the sidewalk.

In the early summer of 1951, when I was twelve, on the sidewalk, someone had slipped a booklet into my hand that pointed me to the door of a new way of life. The booklet had told me I was a sinner, yet so loved by God that He had sent His Son, born into our time-space history, to bear sin away by His death and blood-shedding. He had risen out of death having accomplished this, and was now alive, Lord and Savior. Kneeling in our kitchen, I accepted Him and soon expressed my faith in water baptism.

During the long sunny vacation, I had stood on this sidewalk with a group of teenagers proclaiming from a roughly constructed podium that Jesus was alive, Lord and Savior. Late at night, I knelt on the beach praying with repentant sinners. I had been the group's youngest, physically and spiritually.

Only a few weeks before this November Saturday, I had finally reached fifteen years of age. I pondered the summer now as a gull called plaintively from a breakwater that jutted out into the gentle swell of the river. There had to be more to the Christian life.

I had recklessly proclaimed that Jesus was alive to all who would listen seriously to a fourteen-year-old shouting from an old wooden box. Looking back on it, I felt uneasy. My message had been negative, calling people to prepare to meet God after death. I had picked up a phrase from an old preacher and used it constantly: "There is a hell to shun and a heaven to gain." In the quiet winter months, I realized I thought very little about death. What about now, this day in November? Ready to die, maybe, but what was it to live now?

Over the past weeks, I was wistfully hoping that I would grasp the relevance of the Christian life to the now in which I lived. All who prayed with me cautioned that what I experienced at age 13 in the

Ashingdon church with the Holy Spirit was only a beginning, not an end. Beginning of what? For what and why had I come to know God?

Sitting on the overturned boat, I thought about the previous night; the early hours after midnight spent listening to the dismal serenade of foghorns answering one another, measuring the time between the rumble of the trains that regularly ran between Southend and London along the tracks immediately below my window.

As I turned in my bed, the question had turned over and over within me: "Saved from sin and self—for what?" In the darkness, an inward voice had presented itself to my mind: "God wants to talk to you."

I had rolled the suggestion around and around. God is speaking to me! The thought was ridiculous, a temptation to pride. Me — a sophomore in high school — a confidant of the Almighty! I fervently prayed that the suggestion would disappear or God would teach me what it meant. As I prayed, I drifted into an uneasy sleep.

Saturday had dawned shrouded in the thick grey blanket, and I had escaped from my homework and chores into the swirling silence. Maybe God would speak to me. But all I had heard was the lapping waves and the crunch of my shoes in the wet sand.

Now, sitting on top of the dinghy, I listened again. Would a voice speak to me out of the mist? The cackle of two fighting gulls mocked me from the lonely breakwater.

Chapter 4

Droplets of water had formed on my eyebrows. I got up and pulled my coat tighter around me. Climbing over the stones, I decided to walk through town on my way to my parent's home on the cliffs.

Only a few people were in town, mostly housewives carrying their shopping bags with tonight's meal and tomorrow's leg of lamb. I slipped into the town bookstore. I had an insatiable craving for books, even if I could not afford them. I loved to be amidst the aisles of shelves packed tightly with books, to hold them and scan their pages.

The religious section was squeezed between "Children's Books" and "Gardening." Normally, I did not bother with the religious section as it contained only Bibles and badly written poetry for birthdays. I glanced over the titles just as a matter of course.

One book seemed to leap out at me. It was a small paperback sandwiched between other volumes. Its black binding was clearly displayed in white letters: *Letters to Young Churches*. The title seemed dull, yet I found myself pulling the book from the shelf. The cover was blue, displaying handwriting with a quill on an ancient papyrus. I took in the author, J.B. Phillips. A subtitle informed me that there was a foreword by C.S. Lewis. I had never heard of either of them and proceeded to return the book to its place on the shelf. But I couldn't let it go. I didn't understand my emotions; I wanted to read this book more than any book I had picked up in months.

Almost dazed, I went to the cash register, and my week's pocket money exchanged hands. I ran home through the mist with a strange excitement as if I had acquired a great treasure that had to be examined privately.

The coal and wood fire blazed in the open hearth. My mother was busy making cookies in the kitchen, and my father snored gently in his chair. I sprawled on the rug, my length almost spanning the tiny room. Carefully, I opened my acquisition.

My heart sank. As I opened the title page, I realized I had purchased the Epistles of the New Testament. Long ago, I had tried to summon interest in the Bible or at least the New Testament, but to no avail. The chapters and verses broke up the continuity of thought, and the English it was written in obscured its meaning as effectively as the fog had hidden all within it today.

Each Sunday, as I watched the congregation file into their seats clutching their Bibles, I questioned whether they understood anything within its covers any more than I did. Expensive black leather covers with shining gilt-edged pages held conspicuously in hand; it seemed to be no more than a rather expensive item of dress worn to church.

The only apparent use was to check on the preacher's text when he announced it. But that appeared to be the extent of its function. In the home of one of the church members, I had placed a glass of soda on the solid cover of a family Bible sitting on the coffee table. They severely scolded me for thus desecrating the holy book. My host left the room, and I idly opened the holy book and found that between its enormous pages were old family photographs, pressed flowers, Scripture text cards, and, for some mystical reason, silver

Chapter 4

paper. I couldn't see why a glass of soda could not be added to such a collection!

At first, I had felt guilty concerning my thoughts about the Bible, but I gradually realized that most Christians had never read the Bible any more than I had. It was just not done to say what you felt about the holy book.

The leading elders of the evangelical mission I attended were avid students of the Scripture. They had urged me to read a few verses every day. At first, I dutifully followed their advice. Still, I found my mind wandering as my eyes moved idly across the obscure English of the King James Version. After a while, I gave it up as impossible.

I looked at the book in my hand. A week's pocket money to buy the New Testament. Ugh! My treasure of the morning was ashes in my hands. I stared moodily into the blazing coals and made pictures from the flickering flames. My mind kept tugging me back to the book. Half dreaming, I picked it up again and began to scan it.

The first section was Paul's Epistle to the Romans. Carelessly, I read the first verses.

This letter comes to you from Paul, a servant of Jesus Christ, called as a messenger and appointed for the service of that gospel of God, which was long ago promised by the prophets in the holy scriptures. The gospel is centered in God's Son, a descendant of David by human genealogy... (Romans 1:1-3)

Suddenly, I was fully awake. These words did not sound *Bible*. What was this? Certainly not the Bible I had read over the last months. I thumbed back to the introductory remarks. A new translation by a canon of the Church of England. It had never occurred to me there could be another translation. Translation of what? The Bible was the Bible, wasn't it?

Curious and strangely excited, I turned again to Romans in this little paperback and began to read with excitement; this I could understand; it made sense, and all that poured from its pages squared with what had happened to me. It unveiled what belonged to me as a Christian because of Jesus. I was dimly aware that I had been hungry, for I knew not what, and this was the food that filled and satisfied me. I gorged on the feast. Chapters and books fell behind me as I raced through, devouring all I came to.

The fire embers glowed beneath their ashes as I finished reading Jude, the last Epistle of the New Testament. The clock struck twelve above my head. I was aware that my spirit was soaring with a joy I could not articulate.

In my bedroom, I curled up inside the blankets, seeking to escape the cold, damp atmosphere. The 12:45 A.M. train rumbled beneath my window on its way from London. I found myself thanking God that He had spoken to me in front of the fire. As I prayed, I pursued the thought. Through reading the New Testament, God had spoken to me not as a voice out of the mist but as a voice within. I fell into a deep, happy sleep.

The little translation was the appetizer. It had awakened a ravenous hunger deep within me that only the words of the Bible could satisfy. By nightfall the next day, I had read through *Letters to Young Churches* again by concealing it in the seat beside me in church and reading as the pastor preached. On Monday, I decided that maybe the King James Version deserved another look.

I carried my Bible to church and held it while I testified in the boardwalk meetings. Many of the gilt-edged pages were still stuck together, as they had been the day it left the printer.

Hesitantly, I turned the thin pages to the Epistles of the New Testament, which I had now discovered were the "letters to young churches." Beginning with Romans, I began to read archaic English, its words, thought forms, and style quite foreign to my mind. But the J.B. Phillips translation had done its work. It stimulated an appetite that reached through those ancient phrases and devoured the message.

In due course, I went beyond the New Testament. I ate up Genesis, discovering Adam, Abel, Noah, Abraham, Isaac, Jacob, and Joseph. I inhaled Moses, Joshua, the Judges, Samuel and David, the Kings and the Prophets, breathlessly coming into the New Testament with the Gospels, Paul, Peter, and the Epistles again.

Seventy-five percent of what I read, I neither understood nor fathomed why it had been recorded at all. Yet, as I read, I was conscious of a deep joy welling within me. It was as if a fountain of life had been tapped that sprang up inside me. The words of this book were pipelines from heaven itself.

The leading elders of our evangelical mission approved my interest in Scripture. Some offered me their Bible dictionaries, and others passed on their commentaries. All nodded and murmured their approval at my interest in "the Word."

What do they mean by the Word? I pondered.

All their books helped, but I was drawn to the Bible like iron filings drawn to a magnet. Life came to me from this book that the other books did not supply. I was content to read the words and know the life regardless of the fact I didn't understand.

I returned again and again to Paul's Epistle to the Romans, dimly aware that it contained the explanation of what had happened to me in my rebirth. As I read and reread it, I cowered before its concepts and principles towering above my mind like unscalable rock faces.

"If I am to know what has happened to me, I must know exactly what this book is saying," I spoke the words to myself matter-of-factly in the early hours of a Saturday morning as the 2:00 A.M. from London screeched its brakes beneath my window. It was early in December, and I determined to hear what the Epistle to the Romans was saying before 1954 dawned. I decided the best way to do that was to write it by hand and hear every word.

I spent every spare moment slowly transcribing Romans into a notebook. I found plenty of time. I did not care for sports or the gymnasium, and, along with a few others, I had found ways to cut these classes and rap in the locker room. My new affection for the Scripture now drove me to closet myself instead in an empty classroom to write out the Epistle to the Romans. As the family slept after the Christmas dinner, I was in my room finishing the final sentences of Romans 16.

During the week after Christmas, something happened deep within me. It was not that I had mastered Romans — far from it —but it was mastering me.

Its message gripped me. What had happened to Jesus Christ had been for me. In fact, He had been *as me* in His death and resurrection. His shed blood had wiped out my sin, His death was the death of the old me, His burial was saying goodbye to the old me forever, and His resurrection was my elevation to the heavenly dimension. I now grasped what had happened in my water baptism a few months ago. In that act, my faith had actualized my union with His accomplished work for me. I dimly grasped it, but what I saw thrilled me.

Such a body of truth was the only worthwhile message to proclaim to the world. Jesus, alive from the dead, the Savior of all men. Such a message conquered me, along with all my hopes and ambitions. Before January 1, 1954, was announced by the twelve reverberating strokes of Big Ben, I had quietly given my life to understanding this book called the Bible and explaining its message to the world.

If this was going to be my life's objective, I had to know what it all meant, not only what was there. I decided to go to Bible school. Finding a school that would be remotely interested in accepting me was hard since I was still in my middle teens. Finally, I was accepted into the International Bible Training Institute in Burgess Hill in Sussex.

In preparation for Bible school in the fall of 1954, I began writing out the other New Testament books to understand what they were saying. I was sure Bible school would tell me what all of the New Testament meant.

At that time, I met a blind preacher who had memorized the New Testament. I realized that writing out the New Testament was only one step from memorizing it, and I decided to start. During the next years, I wrote and rewrote the New Testament, memorizing most of it.

I desperately wanted to be in school and decided to go a few weeks early. I arranged to be there by early August 1954.

Chapter 5

THE TRAIN JOLTED and shuddered over the tracks, gaining speed as it pulled from London's Victoria Station. I moved away from the window and slumped into the corner of my empty compartment. Even though it was a hot day in early August, I found myself shivering with excitement. At the end of my journey, I would be a Bible student.

The grime-encrusted buildings and slum tenements of London fell behind us. Suburban homes with pocket-handkerchief gardens ablaze with flowers now bordered the railroad tracks. Stations were a noisy blur as the train thundered through them. The first stop was Croydon, and after that, we ground to a halt at every station.

We finally came to Burgess Hill, a crossroad in the Sussex Downs. Grasping my cases, I stepped down onto the platform. I half expected to be raptured into God's immediate presence the moment I came so close to a school devoted to studying the Bible.

Heaven's anteroom was suddenly very mundane. The train steamed and creaked as it pulled out of the station, and I was left, apparently the only human being in the station precincts. The wind blew eerily through the station arches, and I knew I was still on planet Earth. I had to call the school to inform them of my arrival. A telephone was a new instrument to me as we had never owned one in our home. As I did not have a friend who owned one, there had never been any need to use it. Carefully following directions, I managed to get through, and within half an hour, a red van presented itself in the station forecourt, identifying itself as belonging to the International Bible Training Institute, Burgess Hills, Sussex.

John Parker, dean of students, helped me load my luggage into the back of the van. The drive to the school took us through twisting lanes overshadowed by elm trees. Sheep and cows grazed lazily on either side of the road. I drank in the atmosphere, knowing that I could study and finish memorizing the New Testament in such a place.

We pulled into the tree-shrouded driveway of the International Bible Training Institute. Finally, we came to a halt in front of a large mansion that was the main house of the Bible school. Simple dormitories and classrooms built by the students over the past years were scattered among the trees and shrubs.

I soon discovered that only a handful of students stayed through the summer. I was free to relax on the grounds until September when students from all over Europe arrived. For the remainder of the summer, I was assigned to feed the chickens, geese, and ducks and was assured they would supply many of our meals in the fall and winter. After finishing chores, I wandered in the orchard and the woods surrounding a lake on the edge of the school property. During long, lazy August afternoons, I sat by the lake while dragonflies and swallows skimmed its surface. There, I read my Bible, seeking to receive the flow of life from it. I longed for September, believing that I would be taught what these words meant in this place.

By the end of August, students from all over Europe began to arrive, most of them with a minimal command of English. Lectures started in September, exegeting the books of the Bible and giving information on the major doctrines. The school was very simple in its approach to Scripture—it was the inspired Word of God, His final revelation among men.

Because I had written out so much of the New Testament, the lectures I heard rapidly came together and made perfect sense. I had a further advantage in that I was one of the few English students, most of the others coming from the Slavic and Latin countries of Europe. They were not only studying Scripture but working at learning English, too. I soon became the self-appointed authority on Scripture and Christian doctrine.

When I returned to Southend for Christmas, I walked with the air of one who was the final court of appeal on all sermons, doctrine, hymns, and choruses. I quickly pointed out to my audience of awed teenagers where the preacher and song leader erred in true doctrine. At the Christmas parties, I sat with my New Testament prominently displayed, ready to discuss its treasures with all who cared to engage me.

The Bible school class resumed on a crisp day in early January 1955. As the weeks slipped by, it was apparent that I was miles ahead of all the other students who still struggled to understand the Scriptures in English. After the day's classes, we would sit in the lounge and discuss all we had been given during the day. Inevitably, I was the final word in any conclusions reached.

One evening, discussion warmed, and voices were raised as we argued over the sovereignty of God. I was alone in my convictions, arguing vehemently with the other students. I was shocked. How could they disagree with me? Didn't they know that I had read the Bible, memorized much of the New Testament, and understood most of the lectures while they still spoke hesitantly with French and Swedish accents?

The discussion raged, and finally, Erik, a Swedish student, stood up, his face red under his straw-colored hair. "Ya, Malcolm, I tink you are ze most arrogant man! I haf not met-vat do you call such a person?-ze brat." He spat out the words and walked out of the lounge, followed by three others. The last one slammed the door, indicating their united disgust.

There was an awkward silence and embarrassed smiles. One by one, the other students excused themselves. I was angry, burning inside, determined to prove I was right and they were wrong.

Tossing under my quilt in the dormitory, I realized sleep was impossible. Finally, I threw back the covers, and in the light of the full moon shedding its luminous beam across the floor, I dressed as a church clock tolled out twelve strokes somewhere across the frozen fields.

Leaving the gentle breathing of the other boys in the dorm, I slipped onto the landing and quietly went down two flights of stairs into the kitchen quarters. Banjo, the school dog, yawned, greeted me, and then returned to lie down.

Outside, the night was frosty and cold. Frozen snow lay in patches left over from a heavy fall two weeks previously. The ground was iron-hard under my feet as I picked my way across it, heading towards the lake. Leafless branches were etched starkly against the full moon, and dark bushes cast long shadows on the untrodden snow of the orchard. Thorns caught against my sweater, and branches held me back as I pushed through the naked underbrush toward the lake.

Suddenly, the lake was iced over, radiant in its reflection of the moon from the snow lying thickly on the ice. The boat was overturned for the winter, and now I sat on it, pondering the events of the last hours and the bitter exchange of words.

We had argued over Scripture. Because of the Bible, I had expressed anger, bitterness, hurt pride, and a desire to get even to prove I was right. What happened to the joy and life I had previously received while reading the Scripture? I shivered in the cold and drew my sweater around me. When was the last time I had known a flow of life and joy from the Bible? Over the previous weeks, my feelings fit more into despising those who knew less than me. It was a flow of death.

The Pharisees were men of the Bible, memorizing and studying the part they had. But Jesus called them graves, full of dead men's bones. Their ardent studies only produced the odor of death. Taken up with the words of Scripture, they had missed the spirit of it.

In the silence of the lake, I realized I was more like a Pharisee than a Christian. My mind went back to an incident in Southend before I came to the school.

After a gospel meeting, a group of us sat in Tomassi's, an ice cream parlor near the seafront. Over the milkshakes and sodas, the subject had turned to the second coming of Christ to earth. Four of our group were leaders in the evangelical mission we were attached to and were well-informed Bible students. One had stated that he believed Christ would come secretly and rapture the church away from the earth. The others insisted that the Scripture taught Christ's public return midway through the seven-year tribulation.

Teenaged Christians looked on in amazement as the four Christian leaders raged in argument. I knew the Scriptures they were discussing and plunged into the fight with my two cents of knowledge. As we were locked in debate, hurling Scripture at each other, our waitress asked us to lower our voices as we were disturbing other patrons.

Late that night, as I considered the incident, I blushed with shame. Our Bibles lay proudly on the restaurant's white tablecloth while we argued over them as bitterly as devils.

The incident deeply disturbed me. Now, beside the silent, snow-covered lake, all the disturbance, shame, and questions rose inside me again. How could the Bible, the Book of Life, cause so much hatred and bitterness?

After the incident in Tomassi's, I had watched some of the leading Bible students and had been disturbed by their impatience and anger. One of them had received front-page coverage in the local newspaper for cheating in his car sales business. I had pushed it all to the back of my mind until now.

An owl screeched in the trees. In the crisp winter moonlight, I agonized over the words of my brother, Erik. I had won the argument in the lounge (or had I?), but in my heart, I despised my brother in Christ. I knew the Bible, but it was having no effect on my life. I was left with the residue of a dead, intellectual, heady understanding of Biblical truths.

"My God, I am a Pharisee." Shivering, I dropped to my knees on the frozen sod and received God's forgiveness. I begged to be shown how to be saved from being a student of the Bible and, instead, to be taught how to receive and minister life. I was aware of tears on my cheeks and, embarrassed, brushed them aside.

It was nearly 2:00 A.M. when I crept into Erik's dormitory and asked him to forgive me for being the arrogant brat of a Pharisee he had so rightly called me. He looked at me owlishly through sleepy eyes and embraced me. "I love you, brother, but you must learn not only to study Jesus, but to hear Him, too."

I sat on the side of my bed and prayed, "Lord, teach me to hear You," and realized I was back where I began on that misty morning in November.

Chapter 6

A few weeks later, the school had a visitor from India. He had been preaching in many British churches and had come to the Bible school both to minister and to rest in the peaceful surroundings. His lectures had left me cold and bored, mainly because he spoke in a singsong accent. As he spoke, I had tuned him out, choosing rather to dwell on the current discussion on the sovereignty of God.

It was the Tuesday of his stay, and I was on my way to the dormitory, which was outside the main house. I pushed open the main door and was about to take the steps that led to the gravel forecourt in one leap when I saw the Indian sitting in the weak winter sunlight on the center steps. In his hand was a large Bible in which he obviously was engrossed.

He was right in my path, and I had nearly sprawled over him. Excusing myself, I scurried down the steps and was onto the gravel forecourt when his clipped accent arrested me. "Boy, I have a message for you."

I recoiled at the expression "boy." Frowning, I half turned to him. Who did he think he was? I was no boy. I was sixteen, going on seventeen! The brown-skinned man with greying hair and the well-worn Bible in his hands smiled at me from his corner on the steps. I returned a weak excuse for a smile.

"I think the Lord has something to say to you."

"Uh-huh," I nodded, wishing to be on my way.

"You are not going to hear God speak by studying with your mind, only by listening with your heart." His eyes rested on me, piercing me to the depth of my being. It seemed I heard a voice within, an echo of a November night, and my brother, Erik, saying, "God wants to speak to you."

I had discovered the Bible these last eighteen months but had forgotten that it all began with the concept of communion with God.

"You may be a great student," he said, smiling. I glowed inside, "He must have seen the results of the Christmas exam." But he went on, "But, my son, you must learn to meditate or you will be the worst Pharisee of the 1950's. I have no more to say except you must learn to meditate in God's Word, or what has been life to you will become death and destruction."

He turned his attention to the Bible in his hands, obviously finished with his conversation. I opened and closed my mouth, shocked, hurt, and deeply convicted, trying hopelessly to justify myself. No words came, and he seemed oblivious to my presence. I walked slowly to my dormitory.

The worst Pharisee of the 1950s. Tears welled in my eyes. I was angry. He smiled when he called me the best student. Was he mocking me? I whimpered in my self-pity. Surely I did not need to be more than the best student? I was studying, reading Scripture, memorizing it-what else could I do?

The words of the man continued to speak solemnly to me. Learn to meditate in God's Word, or what has been life to you will become death and destruction. Suddenly, I was terrified at my acquired knowledge of the Bible. Would it all become death to me? I was caught in the same trap as the elders of the mission in Southend. Knowing the Bible better than I did, they left behind a wake of dissension, anger, and bitter spirits. What did the brown man mean? What was meditation?

The branches came alive with bright green buds, and the fields were not spongy underfoot. One Saturday, a few of us decided to go to Brighton, a nearby resort town on the English Channel about ten miles away. Although so close, it was another world. I enjoyed the tangy smell of the seaweed, the grating cry of gulls on the rooftops, and the winding streets with their jumble of antique shops. For the most part, the storefronts did not sell antiques but hideous Victorian vases and furniture that were all so depressing but nonetheless purchased eagerly by the American tourists. I wandered through these stores for hours, rummaging through the piles of secondhand books that could usually be found in some dark corner.

Today, I was going through a pile heaped precariously on a table that had known better days. A grubby piece of cardboard announced them as costing sixpence each. The apparent owner of the store sat in a decrepit rocking chair and watched me over the top of his gold-rimmed spectacles. I pulled some books from the bottom of the heap and, in so doing, partially revealed a worn leather binding with the word "meditation" in faded gold lettering.

The questions of the last weeks came rushing back. Maybe God had led me into this little store to find His answers to my questions buried in this pile of dusty books. Excited, I grabbed at the book and, in my haste, dislodged the whole pile. An avalanche of books slithered in all directions, antique dust rising and choking me.

The old man rose painfully from his chair and, holding his back, stepped toward me. "Ere, mate, watch it, expensive volumes you got there." I apologized, feebly gathering the books onto the table.

I clutched the leather volume that had caught my eye and examined it in the light that managed to get through the furniture stacked in front of the dirty, cracked window hung with cobwebs. Its full title I now saw was *The Art of Meditation*. The author was an Indian whose name I was incapable of pronouncing.

One thought pounded in my head. "This must be God. He has sovereignly led me here to teach me to meditate." Still clutching the little worn book, I handed over the sixpence and walked out into the bright sunlight, strangely excited.

That evening, I settled down in the lounge to read. As I read the title page, it was as if an amber light came on inside me, saying, "Beware, something is wrong here."

I brushed aside the thought and plunged into the text. I found it very difficult to understand. The writer spoke of what he called Atman, the soul of man, Brahma, or the Soul of the Cosmos. The key phrase of the early chapters was Atman is Brahma, or the soul of man is the Soul of the Cosmos; then, man is god!

As the thesis unfolded, it became apparent that Brahma, or God, was the infinite, impersonal, ultimate reality. God was not personal to this writer but rather was everything that exists, the ultimate It.

I finally grasped the gospel of this little book. It was that man must move from the illusion of separateness into the realization of his oneness with the cosmos, and finally, with the ultimate vibration, Brahma, the one infinite "it" that is all.

The way to such realization was presented as meditation. In a quiet place, wrapped in solitude, the devotee was to repeat the word Om endlessly and discover ultimate reality.

I put the book down on the window seat and stared out of the window at the blaze of flowers and blossoms and the sunset over the fields of growing corn. "My God made all of that, but He isn't all of that," I murmured. "You are made in His image, a person like Him. In Him all move and have their being. But, you are not Him, and He is not you," I continued explaining to myself.

The book had only one passing reference to Jesus, describing Him as a "remarkably advanced master." No reference was made to His death and resurrection or to His being the Lord of the universe. A red light now flashed inside me.

My eyes turned again to the book lying open on the window seat. I felt drawn to it and its method of meditation. The fact it presented something so opposed to biblical doctrine did not seem important suddenly. In fact, I found it hard to think about. A kind of drowsiness blanketed my mind. All I could think of were passages from the book like "union with the ultimate reality" and "walk in the wisdom of the Cosmos."

The longing to pick up the book and follow its instructions was so great that it would have been a relief to give in. The thought struggled through the fog of my mind, "This is how a moth must feel about a flame." Then, suddenly, the scriptures I had memorized came back in a blur of truth, cutting me away from the lure of the book lying open in front of me. In that moment, I knew that to meditate as this book outlined would be to deny the Lordship of Jesus and would destroy me.

Grabbing the book, I ran out of the lounge, through the kitchen, and into the yard to the great furnace that heated the house. Flinging open the door, I hurled the book into the flames, shouting aloud, "I renounce these teachings in the name of the Lord Jesus Christ."

I suddenly felt very weak, as if I had been rescued from certain death.

Chapter 7

What did the man mean when he called me to meditate?

Doubts rose in my mind over the days that followed the burning of the book. Had I been too hasty? I rose above the doubts. Although I did not understand why, I knew I had been right. The doctrines of that book were not from God, and my spirit had witnessed against it. But the question nagged on. What is the meditation a Christian is called to practice?

I realized one way to sort out my mind was to objectively study the philosophy I had rejected. At first, this sounded like a contradiction, but I knew I had to satisfy my mind to know why my spirit had flung the book from me. Maybe when I understood what Christian meditation was not, I would discover by comparison the truth. The Saturday following, I was in the library of Brighton seeking out all I could find on Eastern philosophy.

It was not long before I found I was dealing mainly with the religions of Hinduism, Yoga, Buddhism, and Zen. There were not too many books on the subject, but I was amazed to find that there was a strong movement in London promoting these philosophies. There was one book that incorporated Yoga into Christianity. I put that aside, knowing within me that the two could never come together in the life of a true disciple of Jesus. By the time I had finished my studies some weeks later, I was convinced that the religions of the East could never be linked in any way to Christianity.

The first departure from what I knew as truth was the total absence of a personal God in these philosophies. The only God mentioned in them existed in vague mythical and legendary stories. It was the first time I had appreciated the infinite personal God I worshiped, who has revealed Himself in our time and space history through the ages since the creation of the world.

Jesus Christ was not a character of legend but, having been the object of prophecy throughout history, had entered our history, lived in the days of Augustus Caesar, died, and rose again. Hundreds who met Him personally and ate with Him for forty days after His death testified to His bodily resurrection. He ascended into the invisible half of the universe, where He was declared Lord of creation.

The philosophy that knows nothing of a personal God does not know a personal Creator. In these books, all I found was a cosmic "it" manifested through all that is. The Universe is God, and man, too, is part of that manifestation of the cosmic impersonal. Man, then, is whatever he understands God is.

Chapter 7

I had never thought very much about creation. Now I thrilled to the God who was the Creator of a real and objective universe. I reread Genesis 1 with an awe I had never known before. Here was the unbegun personal Creator, who is the life and being of all that is, who, although present at the heart of every atom, is distinct and separate from His creation.

Man was made different from all other creatures in the image of the personal God. He could relate to his planet home and all the animals on it, for he was made of dust like them. But, unlike them, he related primarily to his Creator—a person fellowshipping with Person. Man was not God but was made to be united with Him and have fellowship with Him.

I tried to put my finger on the good news these philosophies were trying to give me. I found it hard to pin down. While sitting at the library table, trying to fathom the object of it all, I met Mark. I later discovered that Mark, a bright-eyed fellow of my age with a full beard and dressed in jeans and a sweater, lived in a flat in Brighton. When he saw my stack of books, he asked me if I practiced yoga. When I told him I didn't, he looked at the pile of books again and said, "Planning on starting?"

I smiled. "The more I read them the more convinced I am that I never shall!" He raised his eyebrows, "Why, I practice yoga." I was delighted. Here was a man who could explain their mysterious gospel.

It appeared that he was familiar with all of the Eastern systems and was willing to explain as much as he could. We sat in a restaurant for the remainder of the afternoon. I continually pushed my question, "What is the message? What is your good news to the world?"

"The universe, including you and me, is an expression of the divine mind. We must realize our oneness with the universe, all other men and with the cosmic consciousness itself. My greatest hope is to be swallowed into it in perfect realization. Until then, we return in many rebirths, paying for our failures and moving farther away from the illusion of separateness to the realization of oneness. In that oneness is detachment, desirelessness, and peace."

I groped to understand what he was saying. "How do you detach yourself?" "By meditation! I am committed to this as a way of life," he explained. "I am a yogi, one who is seeking union with the divine. In meditation I detach myself from this illusion," he waved his hand at the world that scurried past the restaurant windows, "and realize union. Meditation is the way to peace and union."

It was becoming clearer. "What do you mean by meditation? What do you do?" I asked. He went on to tell of a course he had taken in London under a famous guru in which he was taught yoga and the art of emptying his mind of all thoughts, detaching himself from the world, and entering silence. At the end of the course, he had been solemnly initiated into the meditating way of life. He had become a yogi.

Something was stirring, crying out to be said within me, but I could not articulate it. We parted, agreeing to meet the following week. I pondered his words as the train creaked and groaned out of

Brighton and onto Preston Park. We were so far apart. His hope of salvation was found in yoga, meditating with a mantra, and reincarnation. I thrilled to the hope in Christ Jesus and what He had accomplished for me.

Over the weeks, I read over and over the Gospel of John. As I walked from Burgess Hill railroad station and set out along the four miles leading to the school, words from John 19 fastened to my mind. It is finished. It was the cry of Jesus from the cross.

I became aware of what they meant. All that was necessary to bring me to God had been accomplished; nothing needed to be added. Earlier reading from Romans came to mind, assuring me that through the death, resurrection, and ascension of Jesus, God had achieved man's right standing with Himself, bringing us into union with Himself. All was mine as I would rest in what He had done.

The sun was setting in a blaze of gold, red and orange. As I stood gazing across the fields that were alight with its glory, I knew what I had been trying to say in the cafe.

Mark was a yogi, and he had defined that as one who seeks union with his understanding of God. His way of achieving that was his particular form of meditation. His gospel was to attain the realization of union through meditation. The gospel I had accepted declared that God had already brought me into union with Himself through the one act of Jesus.

I turned into the school driveway and said aloud, "Christianity is the religion of done, all done by God. Every other religion is one of doing, seeking to attain God from man's end."

It was too late for the evening meal, so I went down by the lake. My thoughts were alive. Mark had been initiated into the way of struggling to achieve union with god by meditation. I had been initiated into the way of resting in the achievements of another, Jesus. Mark's object was silence as an end in itself, for there was no personal god in his philosophy. As a Christian, I had been initiated by new birth to fellowship with the personal God.

The moon rose as I sat on a boulder, gathering my thoughts. The trees clothed in new spring leaves were etched black against the massive whiteness of the full moon. All was still except for an occasional plop from a jumping fish. The frogs sang their monotonous song from the reeds.

Suddenly, I remembered the books that explained these Eastern philosophies. They all demanded discipline for self-improvement and control. The way of life I had come to in Jesus was simplicity itself. Jesus had said,

> *Come to Me, all who are weary and heavy-laden, and I will give you rest. Take My yoke upon you, and learn from Me, for I am gentle and humble in heart; and you shall find rest for your souls. For My yoke is easy, and My load is light.*
> (MATTHEW 11:28-30)

Entrance into this way began with a promise to do better, but became a confession of total failure and then resting in Jesus the Lord.

Of course, there could be no place in Christianity for reincarnation! One life had atoned for all sin when He offered Himself to God at the cross.

In His resurrection, mankind was reborn at the center of their true selves. It is a resurrection that produces a new person who is in vital union with Jesus the Lord.

> *"Therefore, if any man is in Christ, he is a new creature, the old things passed away; behold, new things have come."*
> *(2 CORINTHIANS 5:17)*

This person has the Spirit of God living at the heart of his personality. No further births are needed.

The moon had risen over the treetops and shone on the lake, lighting up the whole lakeside with its brilliant silver light. I realized the moon is not the lake, nor the lake the moon. Yet, the lake is a perfect reflection of the moon, and the moon perfectly expresses itself through the lake. That was the difference! My yogi friend saw himself as God and meditated to realize that. The gospel leads us to a union in which we are to express God, as the lake expressed the moon, but never to see ourselves as God or God as us. It is a union in which God and man are never merged yet function as one. Paul expressed it perfectly in Galatians 2:20.

> *"I have been crucified with Christ; and it is no longer I who live, but Christ lives in me; and the life which I now live in the flesh I live by the faith of the Son of God, who loved me, and delivered Himself up for me."*

I shivered at a breeze that had come up, and I rose and pushed through the tangle of branches and briars back toward the main house.

Mark was seeking union through what appeared to be endless meditation. I had come to God's goal of union through resting in the faith of Jesus. Mark searched for absorption into the impersonal; I had been brought by Jesus into fellowship with the infinite, personal, triune God.

The spring days sped by. My mind was obsessed with the wonder of the Good News focused on Jesus the Lord. I walked through the week on air, praising God for the marvel of His salvation. I could hardly wait for Saturday.

Finally, Saturday dawned, a bright, fresh day, the sun of early summer making a man want to sing. It was early afternoon when I sat across the table from Mark in the café. A smile flickered around his blue eyes. "Well, are you ready to become a yogi?"

Chapter 7

Joy was rising within me. I wanted to shout. I said, "Mark, I have compared all you said last week with what I believe. I know as I have never known before that I am a completed yogi! I have union with God through my only guru, Jesus the Lord. I was initiated by responding to His faith and work. In Him I have peace with God, within myself, with my fellow man and my universe." It poured out of me like a river in spate.

Mark looked at me, and a flicker of longing flashed in his eyes, but it passed very quickly. He did not answer but went on to explain questions I had left him with the previous week. We never met again.

As I walked away from the Burgess Hill station, I realized that I still did not know the nature of Christian meditation.

Chapter 8

Our classroom, where we spent most of the day, was a medium-sized hut on the school grounds. On the inside, its wooden walls were bare but for a map of the ancient East. On either side of a center aisle were five tables, now piled high with books and lecture notes. Four students sat at each table, bent over their books, preparing for the summer examinations.

We had been studying the Pentateuch, the first five books of the Bible, and I now settled in to follow the flow of biblical history and the unfolding plan of salvation.

I read again the story of creation and, specifically, of the man made in God's image, of his historic fall that plunged the race into death and darkness. The fallen couple received His promise of salvation through the seed of the woman. The promise was passed on to Seth, Noah, Abraham, Isaac, and Jacob. Jacob's name was changed to Israel, and his twelve sons were known as the twelve children of

Israel, the nation who would bear the promise until the promised One came.

From the beginning, the unfolding plan of salvation was based on the concept of covenant; this fascinated me and would continue to dominate my understanding of the Scripture for years to come. It was in that stuffy classroom that I first began to understand it.

Abraham was a moon worshiper of Chaldea. God appeared to him in the form of Glory, calling him to walk with Him and be the one through whom men from all nations would ultimately be joined to God's purpose. He followed the voice of God to the land of Canaan, the place God had ordained as the stage upon which His redemption drama would be worked out. Here God called Abraham to enter into a blood covenant with Him.

Such a covenant was, and is, the strongest bond known among men, the joining of two parties in an indissoluble union. In the Near East, the expression "blood is thicker than milk" is still used. The meaning is that brothers who had sucked at the same breast may eventually become enemies, but men who have become brothers by blood covenant can never be parted.

The details of entering such a covenant vary across the world, but all share the same basic ideas. It is the coming together of two persons or company of persons, the shedding and mingling of their blood, the resultant scar from the flesh wound proclaiming their blood brotherhood. Such a relationship granted them the title of friends. They share each other's strengths, weaknesses, fortunes, and failures from that day. They are, in fact, mutually responsible for each other. To hurt one is to hurt the other; to bless one is to honor the other.

Their relationship with each other is termed lovingkindness, meaning the action of compassion demanded by a prior blood covenant.

The amazing story of Genesis is that God entered such a covenant with Abraham using all the rituals of an earthly blood covenant, enabling Abraham and his descendants to precisely understand what God was saying. (GENESIS 17 AND 18)

Such a covenant between man and God cannot exactly parallel an earthly covenant. Abraham was lost in his darkness and could not walk in union with the Holy One. Abraham was a creature drawing his life and breath from God. He could not give to God anything that God had not already given him. In a covenant between God and man, all must originate and depend upon God.

> *God initiates it, states the terms, and is Himself the Guarantor of its ultimate fulfillment. To receive, Abraham simply believed. "Then he believed in the Lord, and He reckoned it to him as righteousness." (GENESIS 15:6)*

The word "believe" means to say the Amen, to rest in the work of another, to give oneself up, and to surrender to another. Abraham responded to God's declaration of covenant by giving himself away, yielding his rights of independent living, and being united to God by God's action and promise.

God, too, was bound to His covenant. He gave Himself to Abraham (and through him to men of all nations) to be his righteousness, shield, protection, and guarantor of blessing. From then on, whenever Abraham or one of the inheritors of the covenant after him would call upon God, He committed Himself to act in lovingkindness.

Beyond all the immediate and local terms of covenant, the blessing of the covenant was one descendant who would bring blessing to the world. Abraham was being blessed so that, ultimately, the whole world might be blessed.

As I went over the story again, I rejoiced that from the beginning, God's salvation was the proclamation of what God had done as opposed to what man had to do. All man could do was trust and rest in what God had done for him. Momentarily, I pondered again where meditation fitted into such a finished work.

The story of God's dealings unfolded. Isaac inherited the covenant from his father, Abraham, and Jacob received its blessing from Isaac. The family of Jacob (or Israel, as he was now called) went into Egypt, a clan of seventy people, inheritors of the covenant. They multiplied over the next four centuries to nearly three million people.

Chapter 8

They became slaves of the Pharaoh, and according to covenant promise, God delivered them under Moses and brought them to Sinai. It was in that mountain range that God revealed Himself to His covenant people. His revelation described His nature and the absolutes by which men were to walk if they should know life in union with Him. He gave them detailed instructions as to how it was to be worked out—their dealings with God, their families, their neighbors, and the earth God had given them to live on.

It occurred to me that all of God's instructions in this covenant with the nation were totally different from how the nations around them lived. It was a whole new lifestyle compared with the life they had known in Egypt.

Although delivered from the slavery of Egypt and now subjects of God's kingdom, their minds were still programmed to think in terms of Egyptian wisdom. After they had been supernaturally taken out of Egypt, there would follow the taking of Egypt out of them. They had to be re-programmed to look at the world and adopt a style of living that aligned with God. They had to think God's thoughts after Him, think about them until they thought as He did.

They were taken out of Egypt supernaturally. They were to change their thinking by a process in which they were involved. To achieve this, God gave them the Law, the Bible's first five books. They were to make it the object of their thinking and pondering. I was reading Deuteronomy when the words came leaping out at me.

"And these words, which I am commanding you today, shall be

> *on your heart; and you shall teach them diligently to your sons and shall talk of them when you sit in your house and when you walk by the way and when you lie down and when you rise up. And you shall bind them as a sign on your hand and shall be as frontals on your forehead. And you shall write them on the doorposts of your house and on your gates."* (DEUTERONOMY 6:6-9)

A reference took me to Joshua 1:8.

> *"This book of the law shall not depart from your mouth, but you shall meditate on it day and night, so that you may be careful to do according to all that is written in it; for then you will make your way prosperous, and then you will have success."*

So there it was — meditation by the command of God. The puzzle was beginning to fit together. What did the word meditation mean to Joshua? I plowed through Hebrew lexicons and discovered it meant to weigh, ponder, or roll something around in the mind. The word implied such a focus of the mind on the subject that the meditator would mutter to himself about it!

Day and night, these Israelites were to soak their minds in the words of God's covenant, exchanging their thoughts for His; this was Biblical meditation.

The difference between biblical meditation and that of the yogi was immediately apparent. It was not an emptying of the mind but a filling of it with new thoughts. Not chanting a mantra but concentrating thoughts on a specific object—the truth revealed in the Scriptures. They were not meditating to achieve union, for they already were in union. Now that they were in covenant with God through His initiative, they were to bring all of their thinking into submission to His words, and so actually echo Him on earth.

God has not made us automatons, machines that are acted on from the outside regardless of our will or feelings. He never bypasses our reason, intelligence, or desires in dealing with us. He never makes us do things that we do not want to do.

He addresses Himself in the Bible to our intellect and reason. The unbegun Person had spoken to the man He made in His own image. He spoke in the language of man, obeying all the laws of syntax and grammar. The words were put into various books, which together form our Bible. The infinite Creator has addressed Himself to our finite minds so that we may understand the eternal truth into which we have come by new birth. In this book, wisdom and goodness shared Himself with man.

When a mother talks to a child, she uses baby talk. So God has spoken to us using our finite vocabulary, revealing Himself, showing us who we are and the nature of our universe. His ultimate unveiling of Himself and His plan for us was in Jesus, who is called the Word, the speaking forth of God.

God was calling me to submit my mind to the revelation of Himself, re-programming it according to that revelation, and aligning my thought process to eternal wisdom. Like the Israelites, I had been brought out of the world system into a heavenly dimension. Now, all the intelligence and wisdom of the heavenly world must be received into my mind. All its secrets were waiting to be shared.

The Israelites were not told merely to read the revelation of God or memorize it but to meditate upon it! I went back to the Word again and pondered its meaning. What was the difference between reading, memorizing, and meditating?

I was walking on the grounds along the beaten path that led down to the lake, considering the meaning the lexicon had given me. To roll around in the head, to ponder. One of our cows, Leviticus, sat under a tree chewing the cud while flies whirled around her head. She gave me a disdainful look as I went by.

Somehow, her mouth chewing and digesting the already digested food arrested my mind. After she ate the food, she brought it back to be re-digested, re-chewed, and then to become muscle and flesh. "Meditation is chewing the cud," I said aloud, laughing as I did. I foolishly grinned as I sat by the lake. A cow's mouth is hardly the place for divine revelation! In reading and memorizing, I had eaten God's Word—but now I had to learn to chew the cud.

Chapter 9

By the last weeks of my first year, I was excited. God's Word was actually getting into my thoughts and controlling me. But I knew that I was only reading and memorizing. I still was not meditating. Excited though I was, I could find no time. I was so busy studying the Bible that I had no time to renew my mind with the words of the book. I was in danger of slowly dying from an overdose of Bible study and meetings.

I decided I had to make time. I set my alarm for 4:30 A.M. The dawn was greying the sky when I crept into the lounge at the end of our dormitory. The rough wooden floor with a few throw rugs was sparsely furnished with a couple of settees and an enormous black stove in the center, the only heat for the whole building on cold winter nights. I knelt by one of the chairs and began to read my Bible, hoping to renew my mind.

It was three hours later when Peter shook me. "Hey," he said, "you're late for breakfast." I shook my head stupidly and rubbed the sleep from my eyes. So much for renewing my mind! I turned my head and winced. I had fallen asleep with my head in a twisted position and would probably have to endure the agony all day. I tried to get up and found my legs were cramped in a kneeling position.

But I was determined. The next morning, I got up at 6:00 A.M. and slipped out of the dorm into the chill dawn, Bible under my arm. Making my way through the orchard and woods by the lake, I came out into the winding lane that led to Cuckfield, a tiny village a few miles away.

As I walked, I poured out my heart to God. I wanted to know Him, to empty my mind of Egyptian thinking, to be controlled by God's words, not just study about Him. Coming around a bend in the lane, an old church with its graveyard came into view. I opened the gate to the churchyard. It creaked as it had done for many years and, then, groaning, closed behind me.

There was a rustic seat set into a wall at the end of the flagstone pathway that led between moss-covered tombstones, and I sat down, inhaling the smell of roses that was heavy in the air. Opening my Bible, I began to read Ephesians, wondering how I could stop merely studying it and begin to tap its power to renew my mind.

By 7:30, I didn't feel any different, but I was glad I had set aside time to actively reach out to God. He had been the subject of my analytical study for too long. The creature cannot dissect the

Chapter 9

Creator on a theological laboratory table. I felt very helpless as I opened up my spirit to know Him.

Although I had no sensation of a renewed mind, I continued the practice for the balance of the school year. On rainy days, I went into the school chapel and paced back and forth, reading and praying.

The day I was due to go home for the summer vacation, I closed the churchyard gate behind me with a heavy heart. I had to admit that nothing had happened, but I knew of no other way to fulfill the burning desire within me. I knew I was committed to going on.

Southend during the summer months when I was 16 was a seething mass of tired, jostling people. Most of them were what we termed "day trippers" who came from the ghettos on the east side of London for a few hours. During the morning and early afternoon, the shore was empty of men. They escaped into the pubs until 3:00 P.M. when they would either stagger onto the beach or be thrown onto the sidewalk. The mothers, usually overweight, perspiring with tired, whining children holding onto their skirts with one hand and a giant cotton candy or ice cream with the other, stood wondering why they had come in the first place.

The beach was filled with white bodies, which, for the rest of the year, were exposed only to the smog and grime of the slums of Whitechapel and Bethnal Green. They hoped to go home with an angry red burn to prove they had been to "Sarfend."

The air was pungent with the smell of fish. On the seafront, stalls, and storefronts sold the morning harvest of cockles, mussels, clams, oysters, and jellied eels, all raw and served on little plates. Across the street, fish and chips were parceled out in yesterday's Daily Express. It seemed that everyone carried a little plate of shellfish or a greasy handful of newspaper with chips bulging out of the top.

Each day, I joined with the teenagers from the local Pentecostal church and preached from the boardwalk to all who would listen. The hot days on the beach under the azure sky slipped by, and my vacation was almost over.

I was restless inside. Meditation had to be more than just reading the Scripture with a heart open before God. One night, after all the meetings were over and the seafront was deserted except for an occasional drunk or policeman on his beat, I walked by the water. Behind me, the pier lit with a thousand lights stretched out into the Thames. Ahead of me was the beach, stretching into the darkness to Thorpe Bay. The river was dark but for a silver path of moonlight that seemed to span the miles to the other side of Kent.

As the waves lapped at my feet, I wondered how much I had really learned since I had sat here that November morning and had purchased the copy of *Letters to Young Churches* in the High Street shop. I kicked a stone in my frustration, and it ricocheted off a breakwater. I had learned nothing.

I had read the Scripture and known a certain degree of joy, but that had ended in my becoming a student who was a spiritual snob. Now, I was going around in circles, trying to renew my mind. Circles, that was all, and I was now back to square one. I decided I would go and talk with Brother Copsey.

Brother Copsey was a member of our Pentecostal church. His shiny bald head seemed to reflect the glory he had in his spirit. As soon as he entered the church, his shouted hallelujahs could be heard, coming from deep within him and setting everyone else praising the Lord. When he led in prayer, there was a flow of life in his words that was almost tangible even though he was murdering the English language. There was no refinement in his Essex County accent, but his words were pipelines of the Spirit.

To him, the Bible was not a textbook about God but a means of bringing life to people. I happened to be with him when he was praying for the sick at one time. He looked the sufferer in the eye and said, "Listen." He proceeded to read from Matthew 8:17, "He Himself bore our sickness.' What does that say?" And, not waiting for an answer, he went on at once, "Then, where is your sickness?" The poor sufferer winced and indicated a certain part of his body.

"No, it can't be!" Brother Copsey responded warmly. "This says it was laid on 'im. Now it can't be on you and 'im at the same time! So, we are going to lay hands on you and recognize it ain't on you anymore!"

I cringed at his words, my head spinning, trying to follow his logic, but he already had his hands on the man's head and was fervently praying. The man was instantly healed and testified with joy. I was left facing up to the fact that my study of the Bible didn't produce life like that in any area-which meant that I had death.

Late in August, just before I was to return to school, I went to see the old man in the apartment where he lived. He welcomed me, grasping me with his enormous laborer's hands. His little wife served tea in china cups I was certain hadn't been used for a year or more. Then I sat back awkwardly and threw out the questions I had been trying to articulate all summer. "What is the secret of preaching? How do you hear God speak?" I was surprised by my second question. I had never phrased it that way before.

He peered at me over his glasses. It seemed he was debating whether to share such a secret with me.

"Got any books?" his voice growled. I felt pinned to the chair by the eyes that held me from under the massive glowing brow. Before my inquisitor, I felt suddenly guilty that I had ever touched a book, for I guessed what was coming next. He had assumed I had books and ordered, "Burn 'em!" I gulped, searching for words, but I need not have bothered. He went on, "If you want to hear God speak and get a message from Him, you must get really alone. Go to the woods, sit on a log." He was warming to his subject, enjoying what he was saying, obviously reliving the last time he had sat on a log in a leafy Holy of Holies. "Wait on Him with your whole soul. Be still, listen." A laugh was bubbling behind every word he said, his eyes brimming with excited childlike joy. "Listen till you can hear birds sing and leaves rustle." He leaned forward, lowering his voice as if imparting a great secret, "Then, listen to Him. He'll talk to you deep inside, straight out of the book." He patted his big black Bible affectionately. "Then worship Him."

'

I nodded. I had done that. Or had I? He was saying something that was different, as new and exciting as the look in his dancing eyes.

What was it? He continued in a hoarse whisper as if afraid such keys to the Holy of Holies should be heard by profane ears. "It's all in the Bible, but as you read it, you must listen to Him. Read again and listen. He'll tell you more than all them educated professors and their foolish books."

He leaned back and surveyed me. There was nothing to say. I knew now what he was saying. It was so close to what I had been doing, yet a million miles removed. The whole thing was in the word listen. I wanted to argue that I loved books and always would and that our professors were not very educated, and they loved the Bible, too. But I resisted. I had seen and heard what I came for. The old man had unwittingly shown me that I studied and read a book. He came to the same book to listen to a Person talk to him.

As an afterthought, he said, "When you're done listening, and He's done talking, you'll have a message you can't keep in. When you talk the people will get it, and it will work in 'em." He rose to his feet, and the interview was over. I cycled home, seeking to pursue what I had heard.

It occurred to me that I always referred to it as the Bible, whereas it called itself "God-breathed Scripture." (2 Timothy 3:16, 17)

Men wrote as the Holy Spirit instructed, and the idea that that written Word could now be the Word of God to me by an operation of the Spirit made me cycle dangerously fast. God could speak to me as freshly as when He first spoke to the writers of the Bible.

The next two weeks were taken up with preparation to return to school. As I packed my bags, I was aware of a new understanding of the Scripture and idly wondered how I could have missed it for so long. The Bible was not a biography of scholars or students but of 'listening people.'

God was not only the subject of their study, a distant abstraction for classroom debate; He was the living God, the object of their adoration at work within them, willing and doing His will, arresting them to listen as He invaded their minds with His Word. They were not theological chemists, analyzing the Bread of Life, but starving men, eating of Him and so truly living.

I remembered the words that had drawn me to the beach that grey November day. God wants to speak to you. I had missed Him by studying His voice! I was beginning to realize that meditation was the working out of the union I already had with God through Christ. It was the process of fellowship and communion with the living God. My trouble was that I was in danger of looking at Christianity as an impersonal philosophy.

My Exodus studies now came vividly into focus. As soon as Israel had been delivered out of Egypt, they were placed in God's school to be taught how to listen to Him. Facing the impassable Red Sea, starvation in a barren wilderness, dried-up water skins in a waterless desert, or attacked by ferocious desert pirates, they experienced God's deliverance. But the Lord made it plain to them that He was teaching them more than His power to deliver. These were lessons in how to live and how to listen to the Word of His mouth.

Chapter 9

> *"And He humbled you and let you be hungry, and fed you with manna which you did not know, nor did your fathers know, that He might make you understand that man does not live by bread alone, but man lives by everything that proceeds out of the mouth of the Lord."* (DEUTERONOMY 8:3)

The emergencies brought out into the open a way of thinking based on listening to the voices of their feelings, their accumulated wisdom gleaned from experienced life as viewed from the Egyptian perspective. Among these confused and panicking people, Moses, the listener to the eternal God, stands calm, alone, and majestic.

I pondered again the first chapters of Genesis. In his beginnings, man was a unique member of creation. Although he shared in common with all other creatures a body of dust, he was made in God's image to fellowship with his Creator. Unlike his fellow occupants of the planet, he possessed a spirit, an inner ear by which he could know God, listen to Him, and be taught what his five senses could never tell him. Because he was the companion of the Creator, he was fitted to be the lord, master of the planet, to rule it according to God's wise and loving words.

The beginning of sin among men was that Eve listened to a serpent who served as a medium of Satan. She and her husband formulated their own wisdom based on the lie of the devil, rejecting God's spoken Word. Mankind was created as a listener, and sin entered because man stopped listening to God and became a listener to demons and his own confused self.

Now, man's wisdom was honeycombed with lies and distortions, born out of his own guesswork and the voices of innumerable occult devils. Man's understanding of God became a hideous distortion; the creature's guess as to the nature of the Creator exchanged for the revelation the Creator gave of Himself. All that man understood of himself and his universe was based on his evaluation of his impaired five senses instead of the explanation given by the Creator of man and the cosmos.

Adrift from the one voice he was created to listen to, man could not learn his true meaning and significance in the universe.

As my train pulled out of Southend on its way to London and the school, I scrawled a note in the back of my Bible, trying to crystallize the last two weeks since speaking to Brother Copsey.

"The only way man can function as a true human," I wrote, "is to be listening to God and fellowshipping with Him." I stared out the window at the ruins of an ancient castle overlooking the Thames. "By the blood of Jesus, we are brought into union with God, and by meditation, we begin to function as normal listeners to Him."

I sat back and breathed a deep sigh as the rattle of the train increased its tempo, and we sped toward London. It was going to be an exciting fall.

Chapter 10

The first morning after returning to school, I found myself looking at the Bible as a textbook. It was a small comfort that I now knew I should look at it as the words of the Person speaking with me. I began to ask myself what I really knew of listening to people, let alone God.

A verse from the Gospels and the Revelation kept impressing itself on my mind. While teaching the multitudes, Jesus cautioned them, "He that has ears to hear, let him hear." Similarly, the congregations of the churches the Revelation was written to were each warned to hear what the Spirit says to the churches. The fact they had ears did not imply they would listen. Listening was inward and a matter of choice. The sound of the voice of Jesus came to all people, but that did not mean they heard and listened.

Back home in Southend, my bedroom was alongside the London-Southend railroad track. The first night we moved there, I was startled out of my sleep by the 2:00 A.M. train to London. The house shook, and the windows rattled. It seemed as if the train was steaming across my bed. After a couple of weeks, I no longer heard the trains because I had chosen not to listen. The sound was still there, and all my senses still functioned normally, but listening was an inward matter of choice. I had chosen to pay no attention and to sleep instead.

The choice having been made, listening is giving one's total attention to the speaker. One student consistently annoyed me, for every time I spoke to him, he would look over my shoulder, nodding, smiling, and waving to passing friends or gaze about absent-mindedly beyond me into the far distance. The sound of my voice was there, and he had good ears. But he was chasing every thought that beckoned to him. He was not listening.

I recognized myself as being just as guilty! Although I looked intently at a person while they spoke, I realized that many times, I was not listening. Too often, while they talked with me, I filtered all they said through my preconceived notions of what I thought they would say. In fact, many times, I went away believing they had said it — for we actually hear what we think we are going to hear.

One chilly morning, wrapped in a heavy sweater, I was reading from John 12. Verse 29 arrested me: "The multitude therefore, who stood by and heard it, were saying that it had thundered..." God spoke from heaven in an audible voice, specifically meant for the people to be heard as a voice, yet they only heard it as thunder.

How could anyone misinterpret the articulate voice of God for thunder? I put myself in the place of those people. The only noise they had ever heard from the sky was thunder. They no longer bothered to listen to sky noises; they assumed it was thunder. All sky sounds were filtered through their preconceived conclusions. I went to breakfast sobered. When God speaks, some file it away as thunder.

All of this was in the area of humans listening to humans. But how many of these violations of the laws of listening had I carried over into my fumbling attempts to listen to God?

I summed up what I had begun to learn about listening: To listen is an act of my will. Was I choosing to listen to God above all other voices that clamored and jostled for my attention? To listen is to give our whole attention to the speaker. Was I waving at every passing thought and gazing into my yesterdays and tomorrows?

I gave much thought to this aspect of listening. My mind was never still; it was restless yet expectant of God. I took Banjo for a walk in the woods one beautiful fall afternoon. He was old, but that afternoon, a puppy's heart was inside of him. He leaped to catch a passing butterfly and ran after rabbits, only to stand barking wildly in frustration at the entrances of their warrens. A stranger passed us, and Banjo barked as if defending the pathway against all challengers. A passing scent made him stop to sniff the air and linger, anxious to follow where it might lead.

I sat on a log and ran my hand through his thick hair. "I guess I have a Banjo mind," I laughed. I recognized that my mind was like a romping puppy leaping to grasp at every passing idea that flitted through it. My impatient emotions barked at every rabbit of circumstance that infuriatingly escaped doing as I had planned; those same emotions snarled at all who trespassed on what I counted as my rights. My thoughts lingered, hopefully, sniffing the air at every call to fulfill appetites.

How could I listen to God when I was chasing butterflies in my mind and taking time out to indulge in besieging rabbits in their warrens?

But listening was more. Listening is hearing what is said, not what I think should be said. Was I hearing only the thunder of what I had always assumed was true, or what my denomination told me was truth and actually missing the voice of God?

I shook my head wearily. Would I ever know what it was to listen? I prayed that God would show me how to use the ears of the Spirit He had given me in the new birth.

The mornings were darker and colder, and I knew I would have to leave my rustic seat in the chill dawn for warmer quarters. "Tomorrow will be the last morning here until spring," I muttered to myself, pulling the creaking gate closed behind me.

The somewhat ridiculous thought occurred while walking home in a thin mist: I could not describe the old churchyard if anyone had asked me. I dismissed it as a foolish thought now worthy of any further pursuit. But the thought persisted. I had sat among the

Chapter 10

tombstones on a rustic seat most mornings of June, July, and most of September, and the thought occurred to me, "You don't even know what is there!" So real was the thought I almost blushed before my conscience.

Each morning, all I wanted to do was to get to my seat and read. I had seen nothing else. What a waste, persisted the thought. You smelled roses, and you never bothered to see where they grew. The shame clung to me like the morning mist. I brushed it all aside as I walked into the dining hall for breakfast. Who cares what is in an old churchyard, anyway?

Apparently, I cared! The next morning, I woke with an irrepressible urge to discover the churchyard. Once I accepted the return of the idea, I could hardly wait to get to the gate and see for the first time what was really there.

Even before I arrived, I was aware of the road as I had never been before. In the grey dawn, I took it all in with eager eyes. The mist swirling above the irrigation ditches clung in hundreds of tiny droplets like so many diamonds to intricately spun spider webs. As the first light grew stronger, I noted that the leaves were beginning to turn russet and gold at the edges. Then, the wall of the churchyard loomed up ahead, its enormous granite stones clothed in patches of dark green moss. I noted, with childlike interest, the gate. One hinge was bent, causing it to sag. I now knew why it creaked and groaned in its openings and closings.

I found the rosebush I had smelled. It was climbing a wall adjacent to the seat, carefully pruned and tended by someone. In fact, I noted, all the grass had been carefully cut and the edges neatly trimmed.

Wandering through the moss-covered tombstones, I felt their ancient atmosphere reaching out to me. "I could study this place for weeks and not really know it," I muttered. I was amazed to find a number of seats like the one I regularly sat on placed throughout the grounds.

Loud "caws" drew my attention to a rookery high in the old elms on the other side of the church. I had never seen or heard them before. "And, if I came here at noon," I said to myself, "there would be an entirely different atmosphere." I sat down on the rustic seat, aware for the first time of the chorus of birds that sounded from every bush and thicket around the ancient walls.

It was then that the strongest thought formed itself in my mind, almost a voice within, quite other than my thoughts. "What you have done with the churchyard, from this day on, you will do with the Word of God."

I gasped. I had visited the Bible for months, but always speeding through, inhaling whole books at a time, while my mind raced here and there with thoughts like a puppy dog. Had I ever seen what I visited and studied? Had I ever listened?

I had spent so much time investigating the church grounds that little time was left for reading. I began where I had left off the previous morning in John 14. My eyes skimmed the lines, trying to listen to every word. It was no use! By the time I realized what I was doing, I found myself in chapter 17, not remembering what had happened to chapter 16, thinking about the day ahead; this was how I failed to listen —galloping through a daily reading as on a marathon race. I had neither seen it nor heard it any more than I had the churchyard.

Slowly, I turned back the pages and pondered how to listen and discover God's Word as I had done with the roses and the moss. I had written Romans word by word; why not do the same verbally by reading aloud?

I cleared my throat and began to read the words self-consciously. I heard my mouth saying what my eyes saw. My thoughts were drawn into it and stopped their puppy dog romping. I began to hear and see the chapter as never before. I was choosing to bow all my being to what God was saying.

I had to run all the way back to the school to be in time for breakfast, and as I jogged along the dewy grass shoulder, the words I had read burst over my mind, bringing with them a thousand questions that probed the passage and sought what was really there.

"What are mansions? What is father's house? Do you realize that it was Thomas who said that and not Peter? Why couldn't they go with Him?" As I panted down the road, my mind churned out the questions.

The questions returned all day, and I returned to the few verses I had been reading to reread them and pray for illumination.

By the end of the week, I had purchased a notebook to jot down all my questions and the answers that came through further reading of Scripture, the lectures, life in general, and a strange new experience of answers coming into my head at the most unusual times.

It occurred to me that unless we were asking questions, we would not even recognize the answer when it came. I realized that questions were the Holy Spirit's way of opening my mind to hear His answers.

There was light at the end of the tunnel. I believed that I had begun to know what it was to listen.

I now began my meditation with a conscious dependence upon God to teach me to listen. I prayed, "…Speak, Lord, for Thy servant is listening." (1 Sam. 3:9) and "Open my eyes, that I may behold wonderful things from Thy law." (PSALM 119:18)

Reading the Gospels, I realized that although the disciples were seeing the miracles of Jesus and hearing His words, they did not seem to really see what He was doing or saying.

I sat in the lounge one day a week after the morning in the churchyard, reading Mark's Gospel. I came to the miracle of feeding the five thousand. (MARK 6:35-44) I tried to see what was happening through the eyes of the disciples, to feel the miracle happening in their hands. I was shocked to read a few verses later that they had not really heard or even seen what was happening.

Struggling against a headwind, Jesus had come to them, walking on the water. They were paralyzed with astonishment. Mark comments that if they had really seen what had happened with the loaves and the fishes, they would expect such things.

> *And He got in the boat with them, and the wind stopped; and they were greatly astonished, for they had not gained any insight from the incident of the loaves, but their heart was hardened. (MARK 6:51,52)*

One translation put it, "their mind was insensible." All the facts were there, but their dull, sleepy minds had not listened to what God was saying in them.

I read on, realizing that this was God confirming all He had made known to my spirit in the churchyard. I could hardly believe my eyes when I read Mark 8:14-21.

> *And they had forgotten to take bread and did not have more than one loaf in the boat with them. And He was giving orders to them, saying, "Watch out! Beware of the leaven of the Pharisees and the leaven of Herod." And they began to discuss with one another the fact that they had no*

> bread. And Jesus, aware of this, said to them, "Why do you discuss the fact that you have no bread? Do you not see or understand? Do you have a hardened heart? Having eyes, do you not see? And having ears, do you not hear? And do you not remember, when I broke the five loaves for the five thousand, how many large baskets full of broken pieces you picked up?" They said to Him, "Twelve." "And when I broke the seven for the four thousand, how many baskets full of broken pieces did you pick up?" And they said to Him, "Seven." And He was saying to them, "Do you not yet understand?"

Slowly, I read the words aloud: *Having eyes, do you not see? And having ears, do you not hear?*

I knew I was committed to chewing over all God said, listening to every word, weighing and pondering it until I knew exactly what was there.

Chapter 11

As the weeks went by, I found my notebook began to fill with answers and not only questions. I began to write a paraphrase in my own words of the great truths God was speaking in the particular passage I was listening to.

One bitterly cold morning in January 1956, I decided not to venture out of the dormitory building to the chapel but to go to our lounge at the end of the long corridor. The big iron stove was still hot, its red embers glowing under a layer of grey ash. Sitting down in the brown overstuffed chair, I opened my New Testament to the first chapter of Ephesians, which I had begun reading the previous day. I began to read at verse 17. It struck me forcibly that this was a prayer. Paul was praying it for all the believers in the city of Ephesus. I had read it before, even memorized it, but had always seen it as simply part of the first chapter of Ephesians. Now, it stood apart from the book. It was a prayer that the readers might understand the awful majesty of the finished work of Christ. I read it aloud to myself.

> *That the God of our Lord Jesus Christ, the Father of glory, may give to you a spirit of wisdom and of revelation in the knowledge of Him. I pray that the eyes of your heart may be enlightened so that you may know what is the hope of His calling, what are the riches of the glory of His inheritance in the saints, and what is the surpassing greatness of His power toward us who believe.*
> *(Ephesians 1:17-19a)*

I pondered the words; this is what Paul desired for the Ephesian disciples. Along with that came another thought—the fact that it is part of Scripture means that the Holy Spirit desired it for them and expressed Himself through Paul. Then, that being the case, the Holy Spirit desires it for all the church, which includes me! In front of me was God's desire for me.

The transition from Ephesus to me was so swift I could hardly follow the path of my thoughts. I reread it, boldly implementing this idea.

"That the God of our Lord Jesus Christ, the Father of glory, may give to me a spirit of wisdom and of revelation in the knowledge of Jesus. The Spirit desires for me that the eyes of my heart may be enlightened so that I may know what is the hope of His calling and what are the riches of the glory of His inheritance in me along with all saints, and what is the surpassing greatness of His power toward me."

Chapter 11

As I read it aloud, I was stunned. I was listening to God speak directly to me. No longer just great principles of truth, but the Spirit of truth speaking them to me. A joy surged from within me that I could not recall having experienced before. The joy of the living Word laying hold upon me and imparting its life. A historical God to be studied was the dynamic Person speaking to me through His Word of truth in that room.

After living in that joy for twenty-four hours, I wondered if I was being presumptuous. What right did I have to claim the Scriptures as my own? I began to search the Scriptures to see if they gave me that right.

I returned again to the first five books of the Bible, where all truth has its beginning. I was amazed at God's interest in us as individuals, particularly in our first names. He called Adam by his name when he fled in terror, and He gave Abraham his name at the institution of circumcision. Isaac's name was given by God, and He changed Jacob's name to Israel. Moses was called personally out of the burning bush, and throughout Exodus and Leviticus, the Lord is said to speak to Moses.

Their God was not a theory but the living God who invaded them with His Word.

The greatest convert of the New Testament was arrested on the road to Damascus by his first name, being called out of the light. In fact, I realized that John placed the knowledge Jesus has of us at the heart of the gospel.

> *"I am the good shepherd; and I know My own, and My own know Me,…My sheep hear My voice, and I know them, and they follow Me." (JOHN 10:14, 27)*

But although the Bible was a book of God dealing with men on a first-name basis, did that give me a right to insert my name?

As I had gone through the Pentateuch again, it had occurred to me that the promise God had made to Abraham, Isaac, Jacob, Moses, and Joshua was substantially the same, the only difference being that the Lord put their name into it and made it their own. Each generation of covenant men was given the covenant promise as their own by God, who is unchangeable.

I found Joshua the nearest to myself. He came after Deuteronomy and held the complete Pentateuch in his hand. He was assured that if he meditated on that given Word, he could walk out to claim it, acting as if it were his and all would come to pass for him.

> *This book of the law shall not depart from your mouth, but you shall meditate on it day and night, so that you may be careful to do according to all that is written in it; for then you will make your way prosperous, and then you will have success. (DEUTERONOMY 1:8)*

But could I just take any Scripture and put my name into it? Obviously, there would be times when it would be foolish and presumptuous to do this. If I interpreted Jesus' command to Peter that he walk on water as His command to me, I would drown! Nor could I take God's command to Abraham that he sacrifice his son as applicable to all of God's people. After considering it for several days, I formulated a few rules to guard against being foolish.

First, the passage of Scripture had to be thoroughly listened to in order to find out exactly what it was saying. I had to understand as much of its context as possible and answer every question I could put to it. Who said or wrote this, who it is spoken to, and what are the circumstances under which it was spoken or written?

Second, I had to determine whether this was a local command addressed to one individual or people at a point in history (like Peter's walk on the water). If so, God could speak to me from it, but I could not actually insert my name.

But, if it was a passage of Scripture that revealed God's character, His covenant salvation, and promises, then it was mine through Jesus, and I could insert my name; this applied to the promises of Scripture, its commands, challenges, exhortations, songs of praise, and prayer.

I had a new Bible, for those rules meant that I could take large parts of the poetry, prophets, and New Testament and apply them to myself as if I were the sole object of God's voice.

From the day I read the prayer of Ephesians 1, I never ceased to pray it for myself and all my fellow students. In fact, I found myself praying it for people I met on the street. Washing dishes on K.P., feeding ducks, milking the cows, or working in the greenhouse, a sentence from the prayer would well up from my spirit. It was as if I was praying all the time, even though I was only sometimes aware of it.

I realized something was happening in my spirit. My whole attitude was changing, being conquered by the Spirit's desire expressed in the prayer, now joined to my spirit and prayed by me.

The change was also in the fact that I was meditating on the prayer as I was praying it. I began to clearly see what Paul was praying for. It was that the Ephesians might know what they had already received in union with Christ.

The question presented itself: why couldn't they study and find out? And it was then I knew what the prayer was doing to me. Paul assumed that with their own natural understanding, they would not know the full revelation of Jesus, and so he prayed for an operation of the Holy Spirit to do what only He could do.

I followed the prayer of Paul for the other churches and found the same principle. They had all been joined to Christ, but only the Holy Spirit could open their eyes and show them all that was theirs. Man was helpless to achieve this and had to pray for the Spirit's revelation. Another prayer of Paul that breathed the same spirit as Ephesians was Colossians 1:9-12.

Chapter 11

> *For this reason also, since the day we heard of it, we have not ceased to pray for you and to ask that you may be filled with the knowledge of His will in all spiritual wisdom and understanding so that you may walk in a manner worthy of the Lord, to please Him in all respects, bearing fruit in every good work and increasing in the knowledge of God; strengthened with all power, according to His glorious might, for the attaining of all steadfastness and patience, joyously giving thanks to the Father, who has qualified us to share in the inheritance of the saints in light.*

From the eternal beginning of our salvation, all is God's initiative. All man can do is helplessly receive from His unending gifts. Jesus said the beginning of our participation in His church is a revelation. "And Jesus answered and said to him, 'Blessed are you, Simon Barjonas, because flesh and blood did not reveal this to you, but My Father who is in heaven.'" (Matthew 16:17)

In these prayers, it was obvious that the ongoing walk with God is dependent upon the Holy Spirit, opening our eyes to the infinite person of Jesus.

Over the months, I had had only the vaguest notion that the Holy Spirit would reveal truth to me. Certainly, I had never made it an item for prayer. I had memorized large parts of the New Testament, studied it, and sought God in it, but I had never felt helpless enough to ask the Spirit to open my eyes and show me truth. Now, the prayer had conquered me, and helplessly, I prayed that He might show me what the natural mind can never see. I turned 1

Corinthians 2:9-10 into a prayer and used Psalm 119:18. I began many listenings to the Scripture with 2 Samuel 3:9.

In a real sense, this is why I began to meditate. I sought to find life—and then to hear His Word—through the Bible. If I had gone on seeking that without total dependence on the Spirit, I would have ended up worshiping the Bible and had faith in the printed word alone.

The written word is the Word of God, but only the Holy Spirit can communicate that Word to me. To have sought life by a system of meditation would have been the developing of a course in "Think and be like Jesus."

To reason about life cannot communicate it to us. I could fill my head with Scripture and still be dead toward God. I remembered many of the men I respected in the early days, and I wondered if this was why they bitterly fought over the Bible. Was it that their convictions had never gone beyond believing that the words of Scripture were true and, therefore, had not known the Holy Spirit opening their eyes and leading them into the experience of truth?

The Pharisees were men who memorized Scripture and reasoned over it every day while bitterly fighting the Sadducees concerning it. Yet, they never saw the Word of Life Himself standing in every word. "For those who live in Jerusalem, and their rulers, recognizing neither Him nor the utterances of the prophets which are read every Sabbath, fulfilled these by condemning Him." (ACTS 13:27) Even the disciples did not recognize His substitutionary death in their Scripture until they received the Spirit. Then they understood.

Truth is the person of Jesus. He said, "I am the truth." In new birth, I was united to truth Himself and so set free. "And you shall know the truth, and the truth shall make you free." (JOHN 8:32) Now the Spirit of truth shows us more truth via the written truth. He shows us Jesus and leads us to Him in every page of Scripture. Understanding may find the principles of truth, but only the Spirit can bring us to a revelation of Jesus and actually communicate Him to us.

I remember verses from John.

> *But the Helper, the Holy Spirit, whom the Father will send in My name, He will teach you all things and bring to your remembrance all that I said to you. (JOHN 14:26)*
>
> *When the Helper comes, whom I will send to you from the Father, that is the Spirit of truth, who proceeds from the Father, He will bear witness of Me. (JOHN 15:26)*
>
> *But when He, the Spirit of truth, comes, He will guide you into all the truth; for He will not speak on His own initiative, but whatever He hears, He will speak; and He will disclose to you what is to come. He shall glorify Me; for He shall take of Mine, and shall disclose it to you. All things that the Father has are Mine; therefore, I said that He takes of Mine and will disclose it to you. (JOHN 16:13-15)*

I had thought I could still see all with my natural eyes. I now saw that, without the Spirit teaching me, I would not see half. How often had I read, sought to listen, calling upon all my powers of observation? Yet, even then, I was too self-sufficient to call on the Holy Spirit to open my eyes to show me what was really there and lead me into all truth.

I returned helplessly to Paul's prayer for Ephesus and, from that day, made it the prayer of my life, using it every day and each time I opened the Scripture.

In the following months, I pursued the idea of the Spirit being the Teacher and found myself constantly returning to two gifts of the Spirit that I had given very little consideration to until now: the word of wisdom and the word of knowledge. (1 CORINTHIANS 12:8)

Previously, I had accepted them as the Spirit's gifts of revelation. The word of knowledge I had seen as being given to discern a specific need in an individual's life or to understand the true nature of a situation when it would be impossible to understand it by natural reasoning. The word of wisdom I had seen as the Spirit directing clearly into paths of His will that we would never have taken if left to our own reasoning or common sense.

Now I pondered. Was that all there was to those gifts? I had no problem that what I had believed was a valid use of these manifestations of the Spirit, but was that all? If the Spirit was the teacher, would He not be expected to grant a word of knowledge in the course of meditation, opening a text up and giving knowledge as to what it truly meant? Wasn't wisdom, the perfect plan of God spanning the ages, summed up in Jesus? Then surely the Spirit could be expected to give a word of wisdom to show how the plan of salvation fitted together and how history unfolded within His wisdom.

It could do no harm to ask for what my heart was desiring. So, I began to pray specifically for these gifts, opening myself up to the possibility. I added that request to my Ephesian prayer, specifically asking that, while I meditated, words of wisdom and words of knowledge would be operating. Having prayed, I plunged into meditation with no further thought.

Gradually, over the months, I became increasingly aware of a drawing aside of the veil from a text or passage, causing me to sometimes gasp in awe at what I saw and, at other times, to dance for sheer joy.

During the Easter vacation, I talked the matter over with ministers, specifically with George Stormont, who had been a close friend of Smith Wigglesworth. He shared how Smith scorned the use of books and would expect the Holy Spirit to show him the exact meaning of the Scripture, an expectancy that was constantly fulfilled. I never scorned books, but waiting on the Spirit lifted me into a new dimension of meditation.

The wisdom of God, like the truth of God, is summed up in Jesus Christ the Lord. Wisdom is a person, not a system. All our denominational systems of truth are but shadows of Him. If our doctrines are not shadows of Him, they breed corruption and death.

I turned increasingly to the Old Testament, which came alive with Jesus. He was the meaning of the sacrifices and feast days, the true and final Israel, the seed of Abraham. The prophets came alive, for Jesus was the hope of Israel who should sit on the throne of David and rule in His ascension. With the Holy Spirit, I discovered a new Bible.

And all for the asking! I had not had any grand experience. I had just shuddered at my arrogance and asked Him to be what He had been sent to me to be, "who also made us adequate as servants of a new covenant, not of the letter, but of the Spirit; for the letter kills, but the Spirit gives life." (2 CORINTHIANS 3:6)

Chapter 12

In July 1957, I graduated from the International Bible Training Institute. A few weeks later, on August 11, I joined George Stormont to assist him in his pastoral ministry in Leigh-on-Sea in Essex. I could live at home since the church was only a few miles from Southend. It was a painless transition from Bible school to the world of ministry.

The months passed rapidly. It was late November when a church in a fishing town on the coast of Norfolk, Great Yarmouth, was suddenly left without a pastor. I was asked to go and care for it.

The trains steamed and fussed under the vast, smoke-blackened arches of Liverpool Street Station in London. The icy wind howled through the platforms, spinning dirty newspapers into the air. A mixture of snow and rain covered the streets with dirty sludge.

I was shivering, and my hands were numb as I carried all I possessed in two cases down the platform the porter had indicated. Finding a carriage with a sticker labeled "Yarmouth," I climbed in, thankful for the stuffy heat. Fifteen minutes later, the carriage lurched, groaned, and began moving slowly out of the station.

London fell rapidly behind us as the train turned toward East Anglia, the southeastern hump of England. The desolate fields slipped swiftly by the window, the brown earth mantled with a covering of snow. Trees stood gaunt and stark against the white ground and grey sky. Hours later, I was awakened from my sleep by a porter shouting, "Yarmouth, everybody out."

The wind was shining eerily through the station, but it was a clean wind with the salty tang of the sea. I had an address on a piece of paper and finally found a bus that could drop me nearby.

The street the paper indicated was deserted. The houses were joined in endless procession like an apartment building on its side. Street lamps shed dim pools of light every few hundred yards in the winter darkness. I had hardly seen a human being; this had to be the coldest, darkest, most uninviting town I had ever been in.

Finally, I found the house. I knocked timidly on the wooden door, which was opened by a smiling woman. She introduced herself as Mrs. Brown, the treasurer of the church I had come to pastor. Yes, she was expecting me. She had received a telegram that afternoon but had not had a chance to find a place for me to stay. I groaned inwardly. I stayed that night in a Christian guest house in town.

Chapter 12

Although God blessed the little church, the salary never exceeded twelve dollars, and I could not find lodgings. I finally decided to sleep in the church.

At one end of the single-room church was a raised platform facing an ancient stove at the other extremity. In between were some thirty chairs. Beside the platform, a door led into a minuscule backyard hemmed in by towering old houses.

The yard was the only bathroom the church boasted. A faucet jutted out from the stone wall, and a toilet was housed in a wooden shed.

I purchased a sleeping bag and slept in the church. I felt the hard boards of the platform through the paper-thin bag and usually woke before dawn, reviving myself by putting my head under the icy faucet in the yard.

They were among the loneliest days of my life. The congregation were beautiful people, but for the most part, they were very old and totally out of touch with the generation of the fifties. I read and reread the Bible.

In my cocoon of silence, I became aware of another word within me that was a bedlam of noise. I dialogued within, wallowing in self-pity over my circumstances, angry and resentful that I should be treated like this. In the long hours alone, nonsense thoughts danced through my mind. Half a line from a popular song turned endlessly in my thoughts like a broken record, unable to get past one spot. On other days, the key phrase of a commercial would repeatedly announce itself.

"I am a Christian, a minister. How can I have such thoughts?" I guiltily whimpered as I fought helplessly against them.

For the first time, I was alone in full-time Christian ministry and, therefore, master of my schedule. In Bible school, a rigid timetable had scheduled my whole life. I had no choice about lectures, prayer meetings I attended, or the services I should preach. I was suddenly confronted by a Christian world that was a frenzy of activity about which I had to make choices.

"Would you attend our meeting? It would be so good to have you there."

"Could you be at our home meeting on Thursday?"

"Would you share at our Bible study group on Tuesday?"

"Sister Jones is so sick. If you could drop by and see her, I know she would appreciate it."

My meager mail brought invitations. "Would you share a testimony at our women's meeting next Wednesday?" or, "The Christian businessmen have a breakfast Saturday morning, and we would like you to be there to pray."

When I refused the suggestions and invitations, my inner self would look at me with horror. "If you were a good Christian, you would have accepted that," it would say. I stood condemned by my inner inquisitor. The next time around, I reacted to the condemnation by agreeing to be present. At once, my pious self said, "If you were really sold out to God, you would have said no. You are spread so thin these days that there is no time for God."

How did a man know how to control his thoughts and possess the inner knowledge of when to say yes or no?

I was ashamed and dared not share my problem with anyone else. I gritted my teeth and determined to handle it alone. I redoubled my meditation and memorization of Scripture. In so doing, what had been a joy became a drudgery. One thought dominated me, "You are unworthy to walk with God until you have conquered these sinful, foolish thoughts."

Undaunted, I rededicated myself and set about trying to unthink the offending thoughts. Each night, I promised myself I would have a disciplined mind tomorrow. The next morning, I invariably began thinking the same old broken record before I was fully awake. As I tried to quote Scripture in my mind, a line from a commercial would raise its snickering head. As I wrestled with unthinking, my thoughts became fruitful and multiplied.

A visiting preacher spoke on casting out devils. After he was through, I was convinced my head was possessed. But I was the church pastor and too proud to ask for exorcism!

My misery was interrupted by an invitation to be part of the beginning of a new church in the town of Stowmarket. I happily left the church platform in Yarmouth.

After tramping the streets of Stowmarket, I soon found no lodgings there, either. Finally, I was given the address of a lady four miles outside of town in a hamlet of a few old houses, a church, and a pub. There were no buses and I had to walk because I couldn't afford a bicycle.

I found the house nestled at the base of enormous elm trees behind the church. It was sixteenth century, thatched, and had a charm all of its own. The old lady working in the garden looked as if she may have been the original owner. With a heart of gold, she had a tongue that could cut a man in two, and she earned the name the villagers had given her, "the old goat." I was desperate for somewhere to sleep and moved in on the spot.

I was alone again. I hated the stillness of the old house with its twisting staircase and its low, dark beams set in the dead white ceilings. I stared out the window and wished I could hear someone talk, someone to relieve the monotony of the silence.

After an early breakfast, I walked into Stowmarket each day, which took me an hour. After my business in the church, I walked home late in the evening for supper.

The road was always deserted except for an occasional farmer driving his tractor into the next field. It was a glorious time of the year to be on the road. Fall was coming, and the bushes and trees had already begun to turn. Blackberry bushes heavy with the fat, black fruit crowded the road, and crickets sang out the summer in the tall yellowing grass.

But I hated it all. The silence and the loneliness crushed me. I wallowed in self-pity. I was stranded in the backside of nowhere, having to spend two hours a day on a deserted road with no company, no one to talk to, wasting my life in a town that never came alive except on a market day. Since the day in January when I stepped off the train in Yarmouth, all I had known was dismal silence. I walked sullenly past the honeysuckle and hedgerows, longing to be anywhere but where I was.

One dark morning in December, I woke at 4:00 A.M. Nothing stirred; the only noise was the sighing of the wind through the old timbers and the scratching of a tree bough against the wall. December and the bright lights of Southend —I ached for it, just for one hour. That was more than strange because I had always hated parties and the commercialism of Christmas, but my mind had everything out of proportion. I decided to go home. The church could look after itself for a day!

I didn't wait to think twice. Within half an hour, I was standing, breathing in the frosty air on the doorstep of the house. A note to my landlady on the table explained I would be back the next day. I was excited for the first time in weeks. I ran through the lanes, cutting through fields and little woods over the frozen fields, until I came to the main London road used by the truck traffic. It was still dark when I began walking toward London. It was nearly a hundred miles, but my goal made my feet light.

A car drew alongside, and the door opened. A refined voice said, "I say, you're up early. Jump in, old chap, I'm going to London." I settled down and studied my Good Samaritan in the dawn light. He was much older than I had assumed by his voice, dressed in heavy tweeds, his iron-grey hair just above his ears. He looked at me in the semi-darkness. "What brings you to be walking the road to London?"

I mumbled that I was going home for a day. He raised his eyebrows, "Wouldn't it be quicker by train?" I blushed in the merciful half-light of the car, embarrassed that I only earned fifteen dollars a week, and most of that went to my lodging. I said, "I'm afraid I do not earn enough for that, sir."

"What's your job?" he inquired good-naturedly. I groaned within. When people heard I was a minister, the conversation usually dried up. "I'm a minister," I said almost apologetically.

"Well, well," he muttered, "the good Lord must have some good reason for us to be together today. That is most interesting. With the Church of England?" Again, I cringed. In England, to be anything other than the State church was slightly unacceptable; a Pentecostal was quite leprous. I muttered, "No, I'm a nonconformist." That was a safe expression that covered all who would not conform to the State church.

"Jolly good, that's the stuff!" he beamed. "I'm a Quaker myself, though not quite the usual kind. Little too broad-minded for some Friends, but a Quaker at heart. Ever studied George Fox?"

I had briefly and remembered being fascinated, but I had never seriously followed it through. I told him this, and he warmed to this subject, sketching the details of the revivals under Fox.

"What drew you to Quakerism?" I asked.

"It's a long story but, in a nutshell, I realized I was caught up in the whirl of noise. I was like the merry-go-round at the fair, just whirling around and around, empty noise, chattering people, and me chattering back-all adding up to nothing. My head was empty and filled with senseless thoughts. Even church was a meaningless ritual of noise. I felt Someone was trying to get through to me, and I wasn't listening. Then, by what some people would call chance, I dropped into a Quaker meeting house and sat in the silence. That day I realized Someone was listening to me, waiting for me to listen to Him. I have been waiting in the silence ever since." He finished abruptly and looked at me, "Ever felt like that?"

I caught my breath and stared at him in the light coming from his dashboard. Feel like that? The thought flashed through my mind that divine providence and guidance were more glorious than I had ever dreamed. "I have felt like it for the last four years, but these last months I have found out that I feel like it!" Although I could only see the barest outline of his face, I knew I could share with this man; there was a peace, a radiance, a gentleness about him. I hesitated, then asked, "Can I tell you my heart?" I was surprised at myself, having never spoken to anyone like that before.

I told him all, beginning with the turmoil in my mind after I left school to the tug of war between yes and no within me as to where I was supposed to be involved and what I was to do. "I feel like a disintegrated person," I said. And then told him of the loneliness, the awful silence, filled with dark resentments, self-pity, and the feeling of being dumped like a piece of garbage in the back of beyond while all over the world so much was happening. When I had finished, there was silence except for the swish as we passed cars in the other lane and the hum of the engine.

"Why do you want to run from the silence of those lanes?" "I am lonely; I want to talk with someone; I want to be involved in what is happening," my voice trailed away. How could I explain it? I was just plain miserable and full of self-pity.

He didn't say anything, yet I felt my whole person was being listened to. I was not another passenger in the car; we were not just making conversation. I was being listened to as if I was the most important person in the world. And, strangely, as I sat with this man, I felt God was listening to me through him.

"Maybe the ultimate Person has placed you in that silence so that you may have the ultimate fellowship. Whatever you do in life, unless it originates in the silence where only His voice is heard, is froth and bubble. Actually, I find that most activity in church today falls into that category." I didn't argue. Maybe he's right, I thought.

Silence, sure. I had a silent road as I had a silent church to sleep in, but I wasn't silent on the inside. What was silence, anyway? I asked him, "When you say silence, you cannot mean silence of outward sounds. How does a person truly know the silence you are talking about?"

Chapter 12

The sky in the east was pastel pink, and grey light streaked the sky. The lights from a truck stop could be seen up ahead. "Would you care for breakfast, friend?" he asked.

Sitting at a plastic-topped table, we waited for our order. It seemed so incongruous to be sitting there talking about silence in a smoke-filled room with the raucous laughter of the truckers all around us. But that was the point. Silence was not just a quiet road; it had to be more. He had picked up the thread of our conversation.

"How to enter into silence is more than I could tell you over breakfast. In fact, it is a lifetime experience."

The waitress brought our tea, and we sipped the steaming mugs. "Let me say this," he said, "from what you are saying, I believe you need to talk to yourself."

I put down my tea and stared at him incredulously. "Talk to myself!" I echoed.

"Yes," he beamed. "The trouble is that you are letting your disintegrated self talk to you and that was never meant to be. You must talk to yourself and stop being bullied."

The puzzled look on my face made him smile. "You must recall in the Psalms how David talked to himself. Remember Psalm 42, I believe it is? It's a classic in talking to oneself." I pulled out my New

Testament and Psalms and handed it to him. He flipped the pages until he came to the Psalms and began to read.

> *As the deer pants for the water brooks,*
> *So my soul pants for thee, O God.*
> *My soul thirsts for God, for the living God; When shall I come*
> *   and appear before God? My tears have been my food day*
> *   and night,*
> *While they say to me all day long,*
> *"Where is your God?" (PSALM 42:1-3)*

He stopped. "You can almost see the tears on the pages. This man is on his way to self-pity, but see what he does?"

I was amazed. I had never read it like that before.

"He spoke to himself and, in effect, said that his emotions ought to know better! That seems to solve the problem. 'Why are you in despair, O my soul? And why have you become disturbed within me? Hope in God, for I shall again praise Him for the help of His presence.' (verse 5) But then he plunges again into despair. 'O my God, my soul is in despair within me; therefore I remember Thee from the land of the Jordan, and the peaks of Hermon, from Mount Mizar' (verse 6). And so, he talks to himself again."

"If you allow a false self to talk to you, you will be in a whirlwind of a thousand voices. If you will order yourself to be still before the

Lord or, maybe, still in the Lord, you will at least begin to be on the path to being an established man."

Our waitress came toward us. She wore a grubby apron that had once been white. Black rings under her eyes and a bored, empty look made her the picture of meaninglessness. I could not help comparing this dynamic, radiant man before me and the wasted creature standing beside our table. She dumped a plate in front of each of us and shuffled away.

Cutting his fried bread, he said, "Another favorite of mine is Psalm 46. It gives a picture of the whole world falling apart and then says, 'Be still and know that I am God.' I have a friend who knows Hebrew and he says the text could be translated, 'Relax, or let go-I'm God.' That's a command to be obeyed. We must let go of thinking we can run the universe, and rest in God."

No words were exchanged as we devoured our excellent breakfast. He did not seem embarrassed by the lack of conversation, and I felt I could spend a day with this man.

We ordered another cup of tea. "The stillness, the silence, is at the source of our true living." I looked at him quizzically, and he smiled. "God is within you, at the center of you, eternal light in which all problems are resolved. He is the final truth, the only reality in the universe, the ultimate lover who ever pursues us. When we realize our union with Him, hear Him, and allow ourselves to be guided by Him, we are transformed from within."

All I could do was stare. A longing in me bordered on a craving to experience what he was talking about. He frowned, "Never forget this. I have known many ministers and priests in my time, and so many have forgotten the One who called them. They are seeking their significance in endless activity and ritual. Man's significance is that he is the only member of creation who can walk with God." His voice became urgent, and he leaned over the table. "There is only one pearl of great price, and only one treasure hid in the field. Don't spend your life picking blackberries around the field and miss the treasure hidden in it. To turn to that One, the lover within, to yield to Him, submit to Him, and let all of life find its initiative from there-that is life and that is peace."

His eyes brimmed, and the longing within me cried, tell me how to do it. Please don't leave me. Yet, I knew there was no technique to love. I would only learn to know God by knowing God.

"In that silence, friend, much of your activity that you think is for God will drop away and be seen as useless." He stopped, and a smile flickered on his lips. "I suppose such work is for God-the trouble is, it doesn't begin with God! In the silence of His presence all of life falls into place."

"But how do you know," I asked, "I mean, to say yes or no?" He smiled as one would to a child asking for what they would inevitably know one day. "In the silence of light, truth and love, when spirit knows itself joined to Spirit, you know that this must go and that must be taken up. I suppose it would be true to say that life is lived through you. Life is no longer a fretful activity, but a dynamic, fruitful rest."

Chapter 12

The waitress put the bill on the table. He picked it up, saying, "This is on me. The Lord sent you today, and I must care for a charge from the Lord." I couldn't argue; I only had ten shillings in my pocket (about a dollar fifty.) Outside, it was full light now, and we sped down the highway towards London. We sat in silence as I sought to put everything he said together.

Painfully, I have searched for Christian meditation over the last three years. It had been a long pilgrimage that had begun with my becoming aware of a book among men in which God had spoken to His people. I then realized that it was His living voice among us and sought to listen to that voice, depending upon the Spirit to make it real. And now, in the last hour, to hear of a life where all was silent before the One who was within. It all fit; it was part of the same jigsaw puzzle. But I wasn't sure yet how it would fit.

Just outside of London, the Southend road branched away southward. He pulled the car into a rest area just before we got to the junction and turned off the engine. Putting his hand on my shoulder, he closed his eyes. A deep silence descended on the car.

I followed his example. All my self-pity, the failure of my life, came before me. I gave it to God, who loved me and had forgiven me through the blood of Christ. Within myself, I said, be still; rest in Him who loves you. Let go-He's God. I relaxed physically. Within, I dared to believe the love God had for me. The sense of His love welled up until all that was within me was singing and dancing with Him. A living silence reigned in the car. Tears squeezed through my closed eyes and bathed my face with joy. I thanked him for the ride as I opened the door. "The Lord be with thee, friend," he smiled. As the car sped down the road, I realized I did not know his name.

Chapter 13

The streets of Southend were a hive of harassed Christmas shoppers. Jostled by impatient husbands on their annual shopping expedition, a mass of humanity laden with bulky packages swirled around me. The icy wind bit through my thin clothes, and I shivered, thankful for a sidewalk café that glowed warmly in the gathering dusk.

I had arrived home the night before and had visited with my parents until long into the night. I planned to walk these busy streets and take back memories of the activity to Stowmarket. I found myself bored with the streets and saddened for the people.

Sipping my tea, I looked at the mass of humanity that went unendingly past the widows of the cafe. The Christmas lights of a store across the street winked alternately, coloring the street red and green every few seconds. A Santa Claus beamed a plastic smile from where he was suspended above the lights. In the doorway beneath him, a Salvation Army girl stood chilled by the frigid wind. A bus stopped outside, discharging weary passengers to pick up the long line that had been stamping their feet and blowing into their hands for the last twenty minutes. It was all one great façade that masked a tired, empty people.

I ordered another cup of tea and nibbled on a buttered scone. I knew I was as restless as all these people and had trudged across two counties to be here. I knew the Quaker was correct. The cry of my heart could not be satisfied by perpetual activity and masking the heart with constant noise. I must learn to commune with God and be satisfied with Him at the heart of my true self. I would leave for Stowmarket tomorrow at dawn and get a good start.

Over breakfast, I visited too long with my parents and got away to a very late start. There was very little traffic going east, and I walked many miles along the highway. Fortunately, an occasional car or truck picked me up every few miles.

I began to think again of the routine I was returning to. "The backside of the desert," I muttered and immediately remembered Moses, who had been involuntarily exiled to just such a desert for forty years. The silence of the Sinai desert was interrupted only by the bleating of sheep. Before that, Moses had been a prince, second only to Pharaoh at the Egyptian court. From the din and activity of court life to the bleating of sheep and the moan of the hot desert wind through the rocks of Horeb. Why hadn't God used him as a prince to deliver the people? Maybe he needed forty years to be still, I mused.

It must take time to separate the voice of God from all the clamoring voices in the world. If Moses needed to be separated from all those voices to learn to hear *the* voice, how much more did I need the stillness of the Stowmarket countryside?

The road stretched out ahead of me as far as I could see. I trudged on, my feet becoming sore. I ran all of the studies in Exodus through my mind. Viewed as a whole, the deliverance from Egypt and the giving of the Law depended on one man being able to listen to and commune with God. He had then gone from the silence of the desert back to the court of Pharaoh but with the ability and habit to hear the voice of God among all the others who shouted to be heard.

He was met with a mocking Pharaoh and angry Israelites, unwilling to accept him as their deliverer. The immediate response of Moses to what seemed like the failure of his mission was to be still enough to hear what the Lord was saying. Pharaoh's taunts, the aloneness of his one-man mission, fear of what might happen to him, and the whimpering of rejection and misunderstanding were all shouting voices within him. He chose to still them and to hear God.

Being still in a storm of voices was the pattern of Moses' life. Later, when faced with the Red Sea, pursued from behind by Pharaoh with three million Israelites ready to lynch him, he spoke with authority out of the secret he had learned.

But Moses said to the people, "Do not fear! Stand by and see the salvation of the Lord which He will accomplish for

> *you today; for the Egyptians whom you have seen today, you will never see them again forever." (Exodus 14:13)*

He followed this pattern in every subsequent crisis, and there were many! When the people were starving and had no hope of getting food, their tongues swollen with thirst, and their lips cracked from the heat, Moses followed the same pattern. In each case, he retired into the silence within, choosing to look beyond the situation to God and to listen to Him.

My meditation was interrupted by a truck pulling ahead and the driver shouting to me to get in. The truck shuddered, and the gears ground every time he changed them. We bounced over the next miles, shouting to be heard above the roar of the engine. I was not sorry to be dropped off at Colchester. I went into a truck stop there, hoping to pick up another ride. I ordered a cup of tea, got out my New Testament, and thumbed idly through Acts.

As I glanced over the journeys of Paul as he went preaching the gospel, it occurred to me that he traveled the same way as I was right now-walking-and there were no trucks or truck stops! His path led him over desolate mountain ranges and into the plains. He would be alone for days at a time except for an occasional traveling companion. Was it in those hours of silence that he received the revelation of salvation that now fills our New Testament Epistles? Certainly, his first great understanding of truth had been received in Arabian silence. (GALATIANS 1:17)

Sipping my tea, I read Acts 20:13-14:

> *But we, going ahead to the ship, set sail for Assos, intending from there to take Paul on board; for thus he had arranged it, intending himself to go by land. And when he met us at Assos, we took him on board and came to Mitylene.*

I remembered the story. At every city, the Christians had warned Paul of the dangers that would befall him in Jerusalem. He had been bombarded by every rational argument and emotional pleas not to go. He had left the ship to walk across the peninsula alone, picking it up on the other side. We do not know what happened on that lonely walk, but in the silence of those hours, he looked beyond the tossing emotions and arguments of reason to God. Rejoining the boat, he was at perfect rest as to what he must do and was ready to go on to Jerusalem. "It all fits together," I murmured, closing my New Testament and finishing my tea.

A friendly trucker took me on the next leg of the journey. It was late in the evening before my final ride dropped me off at the farm gate I had indicated. From here, I could cut across fields and be to my lodging in about half an hour.

As I climbed over the wooden gate and dropped onto the frozen cart tracks on the other side, I considered this silent world where I found myself. The words of Jesus in the Sermon on the Mount came to me. "But you, when you pray, go into your inner room, and when you shut your door, pray to your Father who is in secret, and your Father who sees in secret will repay you." (MATTHEW 6:6)

God had given me an inner room four miles long, so deserted that I didn't need a door! He had called me to enter, to listen to Him and be listened to. I realized that I had been unaware of the privilege until I met my Quaker friend a few hours ago.

The field was iron under my feet from the weeks of frost. The wind had died away. A church clock chimed out ten strokes across the frozen fields bathed in the eerie light of the full moon. Above me, the Milky Way was strung out across the sky like a million Christmas lights. I walked to the steady rhythm of the frozen grass crunching underfoot.

Suddenly, the words *"The Lord has really risen"* (LUKE 24:34) presented themselves to me. So forcibly were they etched on my mind that I found myself caught up in pure joy. Jesus Christ was *really* alive. I had known that since I had been awakened to Him, but never had the truth been so real as this night. *The Lord has really risen.* I said the words half aloud, then again and again, speaking it louder each time until I was bellowing it out, my head thrown back.

Although the area was sparsely populated, I was sure someone must have heard me. But it didn't matter. Jesus lived and was Lord of the universe. My words echoed across the frozen sod and naked hedges. *The Lord is really risen, hallelujah.* My hands were high above my head as I worshiped the risen Lord. I had never experienced the presence of the Holy One so dynamically as this, not even when I had been baptized in the Spirit. I *knew* Him, filling the universe, filling me, my days, the lanes and hedgerows that made up my daily walks.

Chapter 13

It seemed I saw with inside eyes a world ablaze with His glory. Jesus was alive, and His glory filled the earth. Every bush and tree hung with icicles seemed radiant with His glory. Now I understood the song of the seraphim, "…Holy, Holy, Holy, is the Lord of hosts, the whole earth is full of His glory." (ISAIAH 6:3) I did not have a vision but was seeing from within the way things were.

Jesus was alive. He was here and now. Not merely a sense of His presence, but in His essential person He was here. I remembered how David had said, "Behold *Thou* art here." Not just His presence but His very self. I fell on my knees, oblivious to the hard ground and chilling cold. I sobbed and repeated over and over, "Jesus is Lord."

All this lonely countryside I had plodded through in rebellion was filled with Him — the Communicator, the Word Himself. In my introverted self-pity, I had missed Him, Who was everywhere.

Time, it seemed, stood still as I lay on the icy ground praising God in the language of my spirit until the ecstasy of joy and worship subsided. I looked up, suddenly aware of the grass melted under my legs and the tears that bathed my face.

Someone *must* have heard me. Embarrassed, I rose to my feet. I listened, but all was still. An owl hooted from a nearby tree, and a rodent moved in some dry, crisp leaves left over from the fall. Far away, a dog barked. In the moonlight, I watched a fox scamper across the fields. No one was there. I was alone in a Christ-filled world. The world was oblivious that a creature had confronted his Lord and Savior.

How long had I been there? I tried to see my watch by the light of the moon, but the parish clock began to chime before I had a chance to make it out. I counted as it chimed the four quarters and then sonorously donged the solitary note — one o'clock. I had been alone with God for nearly three hours.

I jogged across the fields to keep warm in the cold that now bit through my wet trousers. Within half an hour, I was sipping hot cocoa in front of the dying embers of the fire in the empty room of my lodgings.

Sleep did not come easy that night, as my mind returned again and again to what had happened in the field. Everything that moved was filled with Him and had its being in Him. (ACTS 17:28) I couldn't escape Him even if I wanted to. I finally decided to get up and read.

The dawn sky outside was a dull grey as I sat by my reading lamp and pondered Psalm 139. I remembered the yogi had told me of the silence he sought. A silence in which he was detached from the world. But there was nothing on the other side of the silence for him to become attached to. Christianity knew of a meditating silence; in fact, it demanded it. But *there is Someone beyond the silence*. I would learn to enter into silence to commune and listen to the risen Jesus by His Spirit and in His Word.

I climbed back into bed, looking forward to my daily walks, knowing that with all other voices shut out, I could meditate and fellowship with God in every fiber of my being.

Chapter 14

I settled into the art of being still and listening to Him who lived within me. My Quaker friend had only pointed the way; I now had to discover what he was talking about by actually doing it. The only way I could learn was by practicing stillness.

I now had an added incentive to silence the chaos of noise within me. But it was no use. My thoughts continued to pass before me like an unending circus parade. Events from yesterday, hopes of tomorrow, the schedule for today, and the tumbling clowns of nonsense and fantasy came trooping past, defying me in my endeavor to be still.

Following the advice of the Quaker, I talked to myself. It undoubtedly helped, but I knew his answer was only part of a greater whole.

The concept of Christian silence excited me. It was not a withdrawal from the mainstream of life. Instead, it was a pulling back within life to plunge refreshed into activity, having listened to and fellowshipped with the risen Jesus.

But how was I to pull back? The dust of a thousand thoughts choked me. Reason and emotion tossed my mind back and forth like a ping-pong ball while my disintegrated self argued over what should or should not be done.

One weekend, I was in a northern suburb of London. I was a stranger there, coming in to preach the Sunday services. After the evening service, I sat with the pastor, sipping hot chocolate before a flickering fire. His wife had gone to bed, and I decided to share my problem with him. He was an old man with a gentleness that coaxed me to be honest with him, and I felt safe in this distant place, far from the people back home in Stowmarket.

I began to talk about sin in believers, specifically, the thought life. But it was no use. The trickle I had let out of my pent-up spirit became a flood in which I told him of all my struggles and failures. "Every time I struggle to stop those thoughts, they fill my head. Sometimes I wonder if I am demon-possessed," I concluded in despair.

There was a long, deep silence, and I wondered if my confession had cost me my ministry. The old man gazed into the fire, nodding and smiling.

"Don't worry, son," he finally said. "I could still have a problem with my thought life, but I don't let it bother me anymore."

Don't let it bother me anymore. I was shocked. Was he saying my desire for a clean mind and a walk with God was merely youthful zeal and a fanatic's dream that would pass with maturity? I smarted — hurt and angry.

He caught the look on my face and said, "Let me explain that! I used to come under condemnation over every thought that came to me. Every time I saw a beautiful girl, I felt stirrings inside of me that reminded me I was a man, and then I would collapse under the guilt. One day, the Holy Spirit showed me I had not sinned by having the thought present itself. The fact I admired a girl was no sin; it would not be sin until I chose to welcome the suggestion, entertain it, and allow it to become a sexual fantasy!"

I nodded slowly, knowing only too well what he was talking about. The thoughts that drifted into my mind or those that came in like a hurricane overcoming me, I had believed that they were my thoughts, originating with me, and that made me a sinner.

He continued, "Ninety percent of your problem is the feeling of condemnation, the shame, for having the thoughts. If that is out of the way, the rest is relatively easy."

I was following him but giving a commentary to myself on every thought he presented. If every thought that presents itself in my mind is not always mine, but the thoughts of the enemy can be projected into my mind, then indeed, everything changes.

But they are my thoughts! They sound like my voice! They feel like my emotions (I stopped for a moment – did they reflect my emotions, or did they bring the emotions?)! Yet, as I let his words sink deeper, I realized that although all that was true, I did not want them; they were the cause of all my anguish in living this life. Surely, if they were truly my thoughts, I would want them, accept them, and justify myself for having them. Was it possible that they crossed my mind but did not originate with me? The thought made me uneasy; someone or something was mimicking my voice and manner of speech to drop an alien idea into my thoughts so that I would nurture and protect it as my own while it sought my destruction. At the same time, it was a hilarious idea that brought freedom just thinking of it!

Momentarily, I thought of the cuckoo that I had heard in the woods around the lake as it laid its eggs in another bird's nest to be taken care of by that unsuspecting mother bird.

The old pastor saw the battle going on in me, and he groped for an illustration.

"Very well, look at it like this," he said, "our minds have a theater where we play out the drama of what we would like to be tomorrow, fantasy dramas of what we would desire in our forbidden dreams. It's the theater of the imagination."

That I understood, and I nodded enthusiastically. The theater of the absurd had been playing reruns inside my head for weeks.

"So, we are presented with a life situation, let's say a hurt. What are we going to do with that? The fact we are presented with a person who has caused us to sense inner hurt does not mean we have sinned; it's what we do with it that counts. Right?" I nodded, dumbly wondering where he was going.

"The fact that we accept the thoughts and begin to write a script only underscores the darkness of the Lie and our confusion as to who we truly are. We relive the incident over and over applauding the drama we have produced. We call that production bitterness and resentment! You follow me?"

I certainly did, and light was breaking through in areas of my thought life that I had never even looked at before.

He continued, "The problem becomes one of identity, knowing who we are in Christ. When we know who we are, we recognize the voice of the enemy through its masquerade and also the Voice of the Spirit echoing the Voice of the Father and of Jesus. The enemy voice produces fear and confusion, and the Voice of Father is always unconditional love. And I am not talking about demon possession", he said with a chuckle. "A rat in the basement does not mean you are owned by rats! But one in the basement gives plenty of problems. No! The thoughts the enemy shoots into us are ideas, the wisdom of this world, and all led by fear."

"You are united with Christ through the Spirit. He said it so plainly that He is in the Father and in us, and we are in Him. In other words, there is no separation, a union you do not bring to pass or arrive at when you have made enough sacrifices! This relationship is the Father's free gift in Christ unwrapped in us by the Spirit. You do not grovel before the Father but, urged by the Spirit, call Him 'Abba' which means in English, 'Daddy!'"

"That is who I am and hear me, Malcolm, that is who you are even with all the crazy that goes on in your head! Every idea of Satan is aimed at blinding you to that relationship and plunging you into a legalism of trying to become who you already are in Christ!"

"When you realize these are not your thoughts, you have not sinned, you are not condemned, you are the beloved of the Father! You are not what the enemy says you are, and you are not the mimicking voice that you have believed is you. Malcolm, you are in this and every moment who God says you are – no other voice can define you. You ignore the foul river that would have you believe it is you and zero in on the beautiful love thoughts of the Father that come to us in Jesus through the Spirit."

It all sounded so wonderful, but would I ever be free? I had them exposed for what they were, but was it possible to be free? "So, do they ever go away?" My hopelessness was heard in my voice, I am sure, but I had to have a complete answer. "I fight them, I try not to think them, but it is no use; the more I resist the more they multiply!"

The old man stared into the dying flames of the fire and then looked up at me. "Never fight them; you will be in that battle for life and lose it! Never try not to think, son, your thoughts will have babies, and you will be fighting on every front. You focus attention on the thought that you do not want, and your intensity gives strength to the thought."

"Put it like this, Jesus said that He is the Truth and the better word there would be Reality. All these thoughts we talk of have no reality until they find a host who will breathe life into them by believing in them."

"Malcolm, you do not fight them but ignore them and replace them. Nowhere in Scripture does it tell us what not to think but rather what we are to think. Not getting rid of thoughts but replacing them with God's thoughts."

"This is not a quick fix! Not one of those meetings where you go forward and say a prayer and everything is changed! Once you know your identity, you will know your opponent and refuse to bow and recognize the creature is there but look right over its shoulder and see Jesus' smile filling the cosmos!"

He slowly removed his glasses and cleaned them with a large white handkerchief, "I get some very unlovely, ugly thoughts presenting themselves to me. I do not become condemned, nor do I accept them or call them my thoughts, but I do not try to crush them, fight or unthink them either. As they float their ideas in my mind, I look directly to Christ who is closer than the thoughts for He is in the heart of my true self. 'I know these thoughts are not mine. What are

You saying?' I then give thanks to Him with the enemy looking on! That's important, son, I don't wait for the stink of it to leave before I praise Him. I am not trying to get the victory – Jesus is my resident Victor and victory."

"Remember Psalm 23? The Shepherd prepares a feast in the presence of the enemy!"

It all made sense, and my spirit leaped within me. I could hardly wait to get back to Stowmarket and see the Spirit work this out in the flow of daily life.

The grandfather clock in the hallway solemnly donged out the twelve strokes of midnight. Pulling out a large pocket watch on a silver chain, the pastor checked the time. "Time for bed, son. Have a good night. Breakfast is at eight. God bless you."

For the first time in weeks, I fell into a happy sleep, filled with hope and the beginnings of joy.

Traveling back on the train the next day, I reviewed the old man's words and began combing the New Testament to see how the early disciples had handled their thought life.

I began with the Scripture the old man had quoted to me.

Chapter 14

Finally, brethren, whatever is true, whatever is honorable, whatever is right, whatever is pure, whatever is lovely, whatever is of good repute, if there is any excellence, and if anything worthy of praise, let your mind dwell on these things. (PHILIPPIANS 4:8)

I had some Greek resources in my case to look at the words they used when talking of the mind.

What I had learned over the few years since my experience of the Holy Spirit was that all the commands of God are not to be interpreted as coming from an angry, frustrated, screaming officer in boot camp! Woven into every command was the gentle Spirit, giving His ability to carry it out. No command of Scripture leaves us on our own to try and do it with our willpower. With every command comes the Spirit's enabling power, wisdom, and insight to bring it to pass.

If I had thought I had to do from my own know-how and strength any of the words the old man had shared, I knew I was back in chaos.

The phrases I found were "take into account," "let the mind dwell," and "set your mind on things above" — another possible translation would be "direct your mind." Let the Spirit show you who you are, live there, and turn it over and over in your mind. When the confrontation with thoughts comes, do not look to your ability to choose or your own faith to pull it off. Jesus shares with you His faith, and you and I trust Him – not looking at our willpower or faith but His and trusting He is now sharing it with us. Our life is not presenting our strong promises to Him but resting in trusting His strength, knowing it is now mine.

My Quaker Friend had called this centering down, choosing to focus on Christ in the middle of the cries and distractions of a hurting, broken world. A centering down that could only take place as the Spirit enabled, not by trying to empty the mind but rather by filling it with Jesus!

It is looking at life from God's viewpoint and interpreting life from that place. This is where all our behavior takes place, and therefore, to have a mind filled and directed by the Spirit is an absolute necessity.

This is walking in the Spirit and celebrating Christ living in us. We can understand Paul in Galatians 2:20, saying, "Not I but Christ".

Chapter 15

As the days and months slipped by, I learned many things about waiting on God. All the lessons I had heard from my Quaker friend and the pastor in London, not to mention all I had learned by myself in school, now had to come together. I learned some and stumbled some, but my pathway was as bright as the sun that was getting warmer every day, thawing the ground and bringing the buds to burst out from the naked trees.

A verse from Isaiah 40 described what was happening to me as I gradually learned more and more about waiting upon God.

> *Yet those who wait for the Lord*
> *Will gain new strength.*
> *They will mount up with wings like eagles,*
> *They will run and not get tired,*
> *They will walk and not become weary. (Isaiah 40:31)*

A lexicon told me that the word "wait" in Hebrew had the idea of braiding in it. That remained a mystery to me until I watched a mother braid her daughter's long hair. Three strands of hair were placed in such a relationship to one another that they became one braid. In a flash, I saw what the Scripture meant. My strength was renewed not by an infusion of His strength but by being braided with Him. My weak, helpless humanity was intertwined with His Almighty Person and became an expression of Him. And the process was ever happening as I waited upon Him in silence and meditation.

I was invited to preach in Ipswich. In the course of the message, I spoke of the Bible being the living Word of God, speaking in our contemporary situation. I urged them all to find time to hear that voice. Afterward, a young businessman, whose name I discovered was Frank, approached me. He shared how he had recently been born again and how deeply impressed he had been by what I had said.

Later that week, I received a short letter, obviously written by one who was used to making memos. In it, Frank simply asked if I was a Christian meditator, if there was such a thing, and, if so, how could he practice it? I pondered his letter for a long time, feeling very unready to share that in which I was so new myself. Finally, one evening, I composed a letter in which I tried to put together everything I had learned.

> Dear Frank:
> Thank you for your letter inquiring about meditation. Yes, it is true; I would call myself a Christian meditator. Your

second question is a lot harder to answer. There is no "how to" in the practice of meditation. No technique can be learned because, at its heart, Christian meditation is fellowshipping with the personal God who makes Himself known to us in the Lord Jesus Christ. The moment you have reduced love to a technique or fellowship to a formula, it has died. We are initiated into such a fellowship by Jesus Himself in the new birth. You indicated in your letter that you became aware of your rebirth, so I believe you can understand what I mean by that.

However, I can tell you what I do and share some lessons I have learned. I am very new at this myself and, so, am certainly not claiming infallibility! You will find your way, but maybe some of the things that have helped me could be useful to you in your personal fellowship with God.

I am fortunate at the present time, I do not have to find time each day to wait upon the Lord because I have an hour walk into town and out again each day. So, the time is already carved out for me. You may have to make time, or you may discover it. That hour-long walk was under my nose for weeks. I was so taken up with complaining about it that I did not see it as God's gift to me.

However you come by it, Frank, there has to be a time somewhere in your day when you pull back from the world and be silent from all other voices so that you can hear what God is saying. We cannot hear Him with our heads full of other voices.

Let me explain my journal before I get down to what I do. It is a cheap notebook that I buy once a month. There is no set order in it, and I rarely read them again after they are full in case I should start idolizing them — we can do that, you know. All of mine are dog-eared and spattered with rain through pushing it into my pocket and writing while I walk in a rain shower! It is a journal for no other person to read in which all the interaction between myself and God occurs.

For me, at this point, just opening the journal brings all my thoughts to focus on what I am about to do — rendezvous with God. Sometimes, just picking it up brings my spirit to a state of expectancy.

The first thing in meditation is to be silent. That is not emptying your mind but redirecting all thoughts to be centered upon God. Don't bother about unruly thoughts; look over their shoulder and zero in on God, who is within your spirit. I have found that praise and thanksgiving are the best way to do this. It is the psalmist's command in Psalm 100:4. In praise, we become sensitive to the divine presence.

By praise, I do not mean chanting "Praise God" or "Hallelujah" repeatedly. Some Christians do that, and I am afraid it reminds me of some forms of yoga where they chant a word, a mantra, to empty the mind. Christian silence is not mindless, Frank. When you praise God, fill it with intelligent content; this may be new to you, coming from your church, but learn to praise God for *something*. I learned this in reading the Psalms. David praised God for who He was, for the promises He had made, and what He had done. I recommend you put all that together in a psalm and write it in your journal. It will pull your praise together and gather your heart to God.

But there are times (not too many) when I have been so cast down that there is no point in going through the motions of praise. The thoughts of despair are so great you can't see over their shoulder! Those thoughts have to be put deliberately under the Lordship of Jesus in the power of the Spirit. That sounds easy, but it took me a long time, and, again, the Psalms taught me.

When David felt cast down, he poured out his feelings to God. Everything came out: what had happened to him and all his emotions. Read Psalms 6 and 7. In pouring it out, he literally took his thoughts and put them outside of himself where he could see them. He did this by *saying* them (sometimes even shouting — do you remember Psalm 142?) and always by *writing* them down as a psalm.

If you try to *think* your thoughts to God, they won't leave you. In fact, all you are really doing is paying more attention to them, which results in self-pity. To pour them out to God in writing is to bring them under control and give them into the hands of God. Notably, in all of the psalms, David ends on a note of praise and expectant faith. He had risen above despair, and his thoughts were stilled. He is ready to wait upon God.

As we Christians understand it, the essence of silence is that we know that we are being listened to by Him and that we are ready to listen to Him. You may remember that Jesus made the two on the Emmaus Road spill out all of their confusion, and *then*, He became the answer. When we cast all our care upon Him, He throws light upon us that puts everything into perspective.

God then speaks to us through the Bible, not just by reading or memorizing it, but by meditating. When all our thoughts are still, we can center on His thoughts contained in

Scripture, turning them over and over and seeking to hear what He is saying to us. I have found that reading a passage aloud many times over greatly helps me to hear what is really there. Then, I write the paragraph I am meditating on in my journal. (You can see why I need one a month!)

Then I ask myself, do I understand what all these words mean? Who wrote them? Who said these words? Can I discover why he wrote it? Who was he addressing it to? Can I find out why he was saying it? Do I know how he felt when he said it? Where was the speaker (the author), and when was this first said or written? You will never have answers to some questions, but until you have asked the questions, how can the Spirit answer? Write all your questions in your journal and cross them off as the Spirit brings you answers.

You must learn to ask questions concerning where the paragraph stands in relation to the *whole* Bible. Learn to look up margin references and always ask if the paragraph's words echo some other point of Scripture. If so, you can be sure it is significant.

I also like to use my imagination to get inside the characters of Scripture. In your imagination, hear them talk, enter into their feelings about a situation, and see it as they did (remember they did not know the end of the story!) Feel their fears and joys, laugh and cry with them. When you read the Epistles, get into the mood of the writer. I sometimes like to hear Jesus talk to me through the ears of the disciples or to be an Ephesian and hear Paul expound salvation to me. It is amazing what the Holy Spirit can do with something like that.

I know that sounds like hard work, but it *is* the renewal of the *mind*! You must understand that it is not *studying* Scripture but holding it, viewing it from every angle, and turning over its passages to hear the Word of God to us. We are waiting upon the Lord, expecting Him to break in with an explanation or flood our minds with light.

One way of describing what we are doing would be that we are holding the Scripture in the light of His presence, waiting for Him to explain it to us. I once visited with a jeweler, and he held up a diamond for me to see. He turned it, catching and reflecting the light from every facet of the jewel; this is what we do in our minds with the Scripture in meditation. Write it down every time He shows you what it means, or you will lose it.

In this unveiling of His Word to us, new thought patterns and a new lifestyle come into being. We begin to live out of God's voice, speaking at the source of our being. Incidentally, I have never heard God speak audibly and only rarely within me as a distinct voice. God speaks through His written Word as we let it open within us.

Whatever you "hear" Him say to you through the Word is yours. You can put your name on it. Turn it into confident prayer. If it is a challenge, you can rise to it, sure that God will give you strength to do what He says. Again, write down such prayers and challenges — even what you intend to do about them.

Go out from that period of silent fellowship and listening with a sentence prayer based on what you have heard. If you have seen or heard nothing, then take a sentence prayer for God's light to fill your mind. Let that prayer rise to your consciousness all through the day. You might carry a small notebook all day because the Holy Spirit will give moments of revelation at the strangest times. Don't be discouraged if you go for days without any sense of God speaking. Keep waiting on the Lord, and He will be your light.

I am still discovering what God is doing in me and through me because of daily meditation in Scripture. God is tugging inside of you to wait on Him. Follow that voice, and you will enter the most wonderful fellowship man can know.

Yours in the risen Lord,
Malcolm

The walk to Stowmarket and back became an ingrained habit. The road stretching out before me called upon me to settle down and wait upon the Lord; I prized that time and guarded it jealously from any other commitment.

One day, as I walked the dirt road, coming onto the paved road to town, a young man approached me with an embarrassed, questioning look. I recognized him as having been in some of our services. He asked if he could walk into Stowmarket with me and ask questions about the Christian life.

I was amazed at the ferocity with which I turned on him. I was like a mama bear robbed of her cubs. My "no" was definite. "I have business to attend to," I said curtly, striding on my way to the village limits and my private Holy of Holies.

Suddenly, I realized how dark I was within. Then, I was horrified that I had dismissed a person God had sent across my path. At least I could have asked the nature of the questions. Instead, with religious disdain and impatience, I had dismissed him. Within me, my arrogant self was saying, "Don't you realize I am on my way to the holy work of listening to God? How dare you interrupt!"

I tried to worship, but I could find no peace. I turned around and ran back to find the one sent to me that I might share that light with him, but he was gone. I finally gave up searching for him and returned to the Stowmarket Road.

The awful truth was plain to see. I was more concerned with the time and the place of meeting with God than with God Himself. But God was above all time and place and could be met with at any time. I had been needlessly angry and impatient in the name of God, Who is love.

All the way into town that morning, having confessed my sin, I asked that God would save me from places, ritual times, and exercises-even if it was the place of an open road. I remembered the man who first taught me to listen in the stillness had so listened to me that I had felt God listening through him.

The lesson was final. I never again established an immovable time that was more important than people.

Chapter 16

It was a beautiful day in late spring. Phil, a friend from the earliest days of my Christian life, was vacationing from his second year in Bible school. He had dropped by to visit with me for the day. We had walked through the woods with the trees exploding in green and spring flowers pushing through the tangle of leaves and grasses. We had laughed over incidents from the past and talked about what God was doing across the world. We came onto the unpaved road leading to the lodging I called home. The sixteenth-century house sat in an acreage that my landlady had turned into an enormous vegetable garden from which most of my meals came. Although she was well into her seventies, she worked in the garden every day the weather allowed her to.

The house was dominated by an enormous chimney around which the roof steeply sloped until it came within six feet of the ground. I had to stoop as I went through the ancient doorway, rarely getting out of the house without banging my head.

I had alerted my landlady, Mrs. Joy, that I was bringing a friend home, and she had prepared the living room. The original oak beams stood out starkly against the whitewashed plaster. The rays of the afternoon sun fell on the dark antique table. Overstuffed chairs and couches were arranged in a crescent around a fire of blazing logs and coal.

As we walked through the woods, we collected sticks and logs. Unloading these onto the hearth, we sank into the welcome chairs. I was on the verge of drifting into an afternoon nap when Phil asked me, "What has the Lord been doing with you these days?"

Immediately, I was awake. The question triggered all the pent-up desires to share what God had been doing over the past weeks. "Since just before Christmas it seems that a lot of things have come together," I said slowly. "I believe that I have finally learned the first principles of meditation and living out from the presence of God within — learning to know God in the silence."

It was an answer I should have explained. Phil was entirely unprepared for what I had said. At the word meditation, he tensed, and when I spoke of silence, he became red in the face.

"Malcolm!" Sitting upright in his chair, almost shouting, he said, "You are going into error. What you are saying is the same as Eastern religions, and they are certainly not from God." He was looking at me, shocked, his eyes almost popping out of his head.

"We had a class only the other day on comparative religions. Eastern religions are full of those concepts — silence, meditation, and passivity. Malcolm, I believe that is of the devil!"

I sighed, "Phil, I know that the philosophies of the East are doctrines of demons. But silence and meditation are in the Bible too, you know. All that Christians seem to do is say what is wrong! It has taken me years to find out what Christian meditation is because Christians have given it away to the East. Do you realize, Phil, that Christianity is the most powerful meditative religion in the world?"

He shook his head as if in disbelief. "You are still Pentecostal, aren't you? What is this talk about silence? Don't you believe in praising the Lord and making a joyful noise to Him?"

"Of course I believe in praise," I retorted. "In fact, praise is part of Christian silence! The kind of noise that must be silenced is the thousand voices inside of us, all the thoughts that come and go. And look at all the activity we are involved in. We call it the Lord's work, but it is sometimes our own activity running away from being still before God. And when we do get a moment to be still we turn on the television or the radio."

I stopped speaking when I heard Mrs. Joy coming down the hallway. She burst into the room with her usual greeting, "Hello, hello, everyone happy?" She was very alert and agile, though her face was lined with the creases of old age. Her gardening and long walks gave her skin a leathery texture. Her once-red hair was a pepper-and-salt grey. She bustled across the room, stooping slightly from her arthritis.

She carried a tray covered by a lace cloth on which was a silver teapot, small china cups, and a plate of cookies. She placed it on the low table in front of the fire. She swept out of the room, telling us that dinner would be in half an hour or so.

I reached into the hearth and put one of the fresh logs onto the fire. It began to hiss in the flames.

"I'm sorry, Phil, I guess I sound like I'm preaching and about to give an altar call. But, honestly, learning to be still and to meditate has revolutionized my life. I'm excited, Phil." I said it almost apologetically. "Jesus is alive. He is waiting to talk to us, to bring our lives under His Lordship. He speaks to us through the Bible when all the other voices inside are silent."

Phil poured tea from the silver teapot. "But doesn't that lead to passivity?"

"No," I said quietly, "quite the contrary. It is the most dynamic activity I have ever known. It is as though vast reservoirs of spiritual energy have been tapped and are pouring out through every area of my life."

Phil sat back in his chair, sipping his tea and wrinkling his brow. I sensed he had finally heard what I was saying. "I really do not believe I know what you are talking about. I have never given any thought to it," he mumbled apologetically.

Chapter 16

"Look," I went on. "As far as the Eastern philosophies are concerned, the silence is the goal, the end in itself. Silence, detachment from the world, is their way of salvation. It is a silence that is only detachment from the world, it can go no further. Christian meditation is *detachment* in order to become *attached* to Jesus the risen Lord. The Christian reaches through the silence to the presence of God beyond, to wait upon Him and listen to Him."

His brow still wrinkled, Phil nodded slowly. I groped for an illustration. "Look, it is like the theater." I immediately knew that I had chosen a poor illustration because Phil did not believe that Christians should go to the theater, but I continued anyway.

"Everyone is talking and laughing, activity is everywhere, right? Then the lights begin to dim, and conversation stops. People begin to move toward their seats, everything settles down. By the time the lights are out there is a stillness and expectation that can be felt. Then the curtains go up and the show begins."

"If you say so." Phil was distant, but I pursued. "Now, Eastern philosophy looks only for silence. Their goal is to cease from activity and let the lights go out, but for them *there is no show to follow*. There is no personal communicating God in their religion. Christian meditation says that there is Someone beyond the silence-Jesus the Lord. For the Christian meditator, silence is merely the preparation for when the curtain goes up-a visit with Jesus."

Phil nodded. "But wouldn't that tend to make you a recluse, a kind of hermit who never faces life as it really is? Always retiring from it?"

As he put his question to me the last months came together with great clarity. At that moment, I knew I could define what had happened to me.

"I have never been so creative in my life." I chuckled at the sheer joy of life. "This is fellowship with Christ. He is the eternal initiator; He is the original Creator. I find that I am alive in areas of my inner self where before I was only half-awake. Things that used to bother me don't any longer. I can meet each minute without tension knowing that He within is my strength and wisdom."

As I considered what had happened in the last weeks, I felt tears stinging my eyes. "Phil, can you realize what it does to the human self to back off from the rat race and hold fellowship with the Creator? It brings about a life under direction — action rising from within where it was birthed by the Creator."

I sat back and stared into the fire. I had been talking to myself more than to Phil. I savored the vitality that had crept into my life almost without my realizing it. Phil interrupted my reverie. "Do you have such a living experience all the time?" It was an honest question with no hint of sarcasm. I pondered the last weeks. I remembered hours when I had experienced no unusual sense of God, hours spent pondering, weighing, questioning the Scripture, and coming away with no sense of having heard God speak. But then there were those days when His presence was so real He could almost be touched, and in those moments, all the dry hours would bring forth fruit. Light and understanding would then flash into my mind, and I could honestly say that God had spoken to me through His Word.

I answered Phil slowly. "No, I sometimes go for a couple of weeks just waiting, listening in the Bible. Then, for no reason I have been able to explain, suddenly everything lights up." As I spoke, I realized why I did not have a continual revelation and said, "It is God we are waiting on, not the *experience* of Him. If we felt Him all the time, we would worship the feeling and end up idolizing the man who consistently had those feelings!"

Phil nodded. "You know, Malcolm, during the past months in school I believe I have lost that personal knowledge of God I once had. Isn't that incredible? I am a student of Pentecostal theology, yet God as a *living person* is quite remote from me. He stopped with a choke in his voice. Regaining his composure, he said hoarsely, "Oh, I can tell you how to prepare a sermon and how to preach it. If you want to understand Genesis, I can give you an outline. But I am a shriveled man on the inside. Thanks for sharing what you have. I believe God led us into this conversation." Tears brimmed in his eyes as he looked into the fire.

His words brought back a replay of memories. A brown man sitting on the steps of another Bible school calling out to an arrogant honor student, warning him that he might become the worst Pharisee of the 1950s. I silently praised God that He had led me on the path of knowing Him in this personal way and prayed Phil would be similarly led.

The firelight flickered on our faces in the twilight, but a great light shone inside us. Alone yet together, we waited on God, transfixed in the living sense of His presence.

The rasping voice of the landlady called from the kitchen that dinner was ready. Two renewed men moved to the table.

Chapter 17

WHILE PASTORING IN STOWMARKET, I was married and very soon afterward moved to London. Using our apartment as a home base, I traveled throughout the British Isles, preaching in churches of all denominations.

It rapidly became apparent that Stowmarket and London were two separate worlds. I no longer had a deserted road on which to rendezvous with God each day. No more the crystal silence of a winter night under a sky ablaze with stars or the drone of a bee visiting roadside flowers on a lazy summer afternoon. Instead, I was in a dismal city draped with smog and grime. The dull roar of traffic was the uninterrupted backdrop of life.

Traveling from city to city, I spent many hours in sooty railroad stations or jammed into stuffy cars that rocked and swayed as they thundered through the night into Scotland or Wales. I could still center down and commune with God in the midst of it all, but I felt a certain emptiness within me as if something had been lost. I sometimes wondered where meditation fit into all of this. I could hardly define what I was missing, so I dismissed the problem.

Our first daughter, Donna, was born in London, and shortly after that, I received an invitation to preach for a week of meetings in Belfast, Northern Ireland.

In Ulster, the British-controlled north of Ireland, I felt I had stepped out of a time machine into the early 1900's. I did not complain but welcomed a return to the slow pace after the mad rush of London. During the week of preaching in Belfast, I received invitations to minister throughout the province, and after a brief return to collect our things, we went to live in Ireland.

After a few months of traveling through the churches in Ireland, I was called by a Pentecostal church in Armagh City to be their pastor. The charge consisted of the city church and a small branch work in the outlying district of Market Hill. I accepted the call. Immediately, I was plunged into a schedule that included preaching a full Sunday of morning and evening services in both churches and visiting the members scattered for miles over the County Armagh countryside. After I had been there a few weeks, the superintendent of the Irish Pentecostal churches asked me to add to my pastoral duties the leadership of all the youth of that denomination. I accepted and found myself back on the road each Saturday, conducting youth rallies throughout Ulster.

One particular Monday — as I sat exhausted in my study in Armagh, the giant oak table that served as my desk strewn with sermon notes, letters to be answered, and administrative papers connected with the youth organization — the red notebook caught my attention. I had purchased it to be my latest journal four weeks previously. Its pages were uncreased, crisp, and clean. Its empty pages were the mirror of my spirit. I was so caught up in doing God's work that I had no time for fellowship with God.

I knew that I had to take drastic action. My schedule had no spare hours, so I knew I had to *find* or *make* time. "Jesus was much busier than you," I reminded myself, "and He found time for long hours of fellowship with God!" I decided then and there to *put* time into my day by rising an hour earlier.

But that was not enough. With the many meetings that filled my weeks, I knew I needed extra time to be still and wait upon God to bring all my comings and goings to His light. I decided to take one full day a month and reserve it for being alone with God.

I pulled my duffle coat around me, hunching my shoulders against the buffeting wind. A fine mist skimmed from the top of the whitecaps far out from the shore, stinging my face to a glow. I took it all in around me — the low roar of the Atlantic surf from further down the beach, the dark clouds on the horizon and scudding rapidly across the overcast sky, and the fresh smell of a storm in November.

My watch told me it was ten o'clock, soon time for lunch. I must have been walking on the sand for about half an hour. Four hours earlier, I had backed the ancient 1939 church car out of our driveway and driven through Ulster, crossing the border in Eire just outside of Londonderry.

I had chosen these bleak beaches of Donegal for the first Sabbath waiting upon God. I now wrestled with the problem that had bothered me in London. Whatever caused the empty feeling probably caused me to gradually almost stop the practice of meditation in the past weeks. The hours I had in Stowmarket to wait on God in silence was a luxury very few could have. I certainly did not have it anymore and did not suppose I ever would again. I had to find what was lacking in my meditation since those days.

Since leaving Stowmarket, there has been no change in what I did. What more could I do? As I had driven that morning and tramped along the beach, I tried to stand back and ask myself what was wrong. Looking at it objectively, I saw the time of stillness as an entity itself. It stood there isolated, the quiet hour. Indeed, it spoke to all my life. From it, creativity flowed, and a certain quality of stillness was given to all the other hours. But essentially, it was unrelated to the whirling schedule that I was caught up in and so had taken on a kind of unreality. "That's it!" I murmured triumphantly. "An hour with God has become almost a fantasy hour!" It had fit into the Bible school atmosphere and also the sleepy lanes around Stowmarket, but in the rush of life, it stood stark and alone, not part of where my real life was.

My shoes crunched in the tightly packed sand left by the receding tide. Piles of rocks sprawled along the beach as if tossed there by a giant hand. The wind gusted through them, singing a melancholy dirge in a minor key.

"Yet," I argued with myself, "actually, it is quite the reverse. The ultimate reality *is* fellowshipping with the risen Jesus!"

I was beside the water now, the foam of breaking waves swirling a few inches from my feet before receding, leaving hundreds of little foam bubbles to show it had been there.

"Lord, that's the mad, whirling world," I prayed. "It is here today, gone tomorrow, and leaves only a few bubbles to show it had ever been at all. By comparison, my fellowship with you is like those rocks." Yet, how did I bring that reality into my life?

I was getting hungry and was glad to discover a cove, a natural harbor sheltered from the unrelenting fury of the gale. The wind and waves were a muffled roar from within the horseshoe of the cove.

All was still. Seagulls crouched low on the sand, waiting out the ferocity of the wind. They looked at me with hostile eyes as I sat down against the cliff face. I had brought my lunch in an old bag slung over my shoulder. I pulled out a flask and poured a cup of steaming tea. It warmed me as I sipped it gratefully. I took out my Bible and turned to Joshua 1:8, reading it slowly.

> *This book of the law shall not depart from your mouth, but*
> *you shall meditate on it day and night, so that you may be*
> *careful to do according to all that is written in it; for then*

you will make your way prosperous, and then you will have success.

It had been the Scripture that had first introduced me to Christian meditation. I returned now to find answers to the questions that reached out inside me. The words "be careful to do" arrested me. I had always understood that meditating meant doing and being what God called us to be. Today, the words stood out, demanding that I hear them afresh.

Be careful to do. I had undoubtedly done a lot of observing of the Scripture. Although my life had felt that impact, these words challenged me with something more. It reminded me that in the Scripture and by His Spirit within me, God addressed Himself to my mind, calling upon *me* to change my actions and conform to His truth.

I gasped at the implication. God will never change us without our permission. He will never move into our lives if we don't want Him to. Man is not an automaton, a machine that God acts on from the outside. In the process of changing us to the image of Jesus, He does not bypass our will, feelings, reason, or intelligence. He directs His Word in the power of the Spirit to our whole person and then calls upon us to choose to do it.

My mind went back to my first studies in meditation to the way God had taken Israel out of Egypt by His power and Egypt out of them by His Word. They came out of the world system and, faced with God's truth, were told to meditate and *do* it.

The world system I came out of was no different. Its standards, the body of facts it called wisdom, and its goals and ambitions were all based on the original lie that man was at the center of the universe.

After being born again, I had not realized how much of the world's wisdom and attitudes were lodged within me. Meditation gradually introduced me to a whole new value system based on God's truth. I had already realized that God was not who I had thought He was, and I was not the man I had believed myself to be. Confronting the risen Jesus in the silence demanded an ongoing change. But that change had not really affected too much of what I did. Reading from Joshua, I realized that whenever the world system had a foot in my door, whether its practices or what it termed wisdom, it would have to be challenged by the truth I meditated on.

I poured another cup of tea and munched on a sandwich. I remembered verses I had memorized from the Epistles that described meditation, bringing out this aspect of it–"Knowledge of the truth" (2 TIMOTHY 2:25) and "Obedience to the truth purified your souls." (2 PETER 1:22)

Over the months, I had been delighting in the truth as I observed it, which certainly had a great effect on me. But this morning, sipping my tea near a rock on the sands of Donegal, I heard His Word say *do* it. All my life habits, involvements, and non-involvements had to be challenged by the truth.

The chill air finally penetrated my heavy coat and sweater, and I pulled myself to my feet. As I brushed the sand from my clothes, I was aware of an excitement deep within me.

I had been walking in the midst of a world system, aware that I was on the outside of it. That was the extent of my Christianity, a list of what I was not. I realized that my activity as a Christian could be defined by the things I did *not* do and the places I did *not* frequent. Worse yet, I had no rationale for those negatives except that the denomination demanded them. I was a ghost in the world, a man who *did not*. No wonder fellowshipping with God seemed unreal, for I had not related it to the actual living of life in the real world. It had come dangerously close to being a spiritual hobby!

That morning, the Holy Spirit showed me that God's Word had to be aggressively applied by me to every area of life. I had to be the man who *did* what God said, not merely one who *did not* do what the world did. I felt as though I was emerging from a ghost world into the real world of Him who said, "I am the truth."

The gulls became disturbed as I walked toward them. "Probably, I am the first human they have encountered in a week," I mused. They struggled to their feet, ran a few ungainly steps, and, flapping their great wings, became momentarily airborne only to land a few feet away. They crouched on the sand again, eyeing me suspiciously.

Ever since my Bible school days, I had personalized the Scripture, making it my own, but I had not felt the thrust of His demand upon me as I did now. The Scripture was His truth addressed to *me*, challenging *me* to align myself to it in every circumstance and all my attitudes. Until now, I had vaguely believed that God would somehow align me to Himself. Now I knew that my light and strength within demanded that *I* choose to walk according to truth.

As I walked between the sand dunes back to the car, my mind turned to Genesis 1. I had recently discovered an arresting picture in the first verses. The process of creation was described as a combination of the Holy Spirit moving and the Word of God *speaking*.

In the Hebrew language, the expression "moving" could be translated as "brooding" or "fluttering," as a mother hen does over her fertile eggs. It gave the picture of the Holy Spirit as brooding over the living Word God had spoken and *hatching* it into being. I saw now that meditation was the process of taking God's Word, holding it in the creative light of the Spirit, and bringing my whole life to submit to it in the power of the Spirit as my choices were made in that light so that the Word would hatch into a new lifestyle.

As I drove back across County Fermanagh, a full moon rode high in the nearly cloudless sky. I looked out over the peat bogs and rolling hills. Inside, I was exhilarated. I knew that a new dimension of meditation had opened up to me.

Chapter 18

Pulling back from the rush and waiting on the Lord one day a month produced results immediately. The little church in Market Hill began to fill with people and soon was too small to hold the crowds that jammed into it. Among the crowds was a butcher, Bob Flanagan, who was revived in his Christian experience through the services.

The youth meetings took me all over Ireland. In my preaching, I emphasized the work of the Holy Spirit to the hundreds of people who gathered in churches and auditoriums. Someone remarked in one of these meetings that I should go to the United States. I had always wanted to go but never thought seriously about it. Lack of funds made it an impossible idea.

A few weeks after the suggestion was made, I was preaching in Belfast. After the meeting, a tall, lanky fellow in a light blue suit approached me and gave me his card. He was a pastor from a

Pentecostal church in Alberta, Canada. He assured me that if I came to North America, no church would be big enough to hold the people who would come. I didn't need to hear that; my present crowds were the biggest I had preached to. It was heady wine for a young man in his early twenties. I began to anticipate my future great crusades.

A month later, there was a timid knock on our front door. It was Bob Flanagan, the butcher. He shifted awkwardly from foot to foot, turning his cap around in his hand. He did not look at me but kept his eyes trained on my shoes.

In his Irish country dialect, he blurted out, "The Lord's been speaking to me last night, so I couldn't sleep. When I was away from God, I never gave tithes. I made up all my back tithes last Sunday, but last night, I was convicted that I should give more and give it to you." Red-faced, he thrust an envelope into my hands and fled to his car.

Mystified, I opened the envelope as his car sped away. Inside were four hundred pounds in crisp new notes. In those days, it was around a thousand dollars. At once, I accepted it as the fare to Canada. I should have recognized the misgiving that nagged deep within me.

It was only a couple of hours before the family was in the car and driving the road to Belfast to book the tickets. All I could think of was that this had to be God — first, an invitation, and now the money to go. The agent was very helpful and gave us the best she could for the thousand dollars. She pushed the tickets across the desk, and I handed her the money.

At that moment, I knew I was wrong. The One, who was within my spirit, immediately made it known to me, not by process of reason, but by His intuitive voice in the light. Within, I was excited and happy, reasoning that everything fitted together so perfectly in God's timing. But, at the center of my being, the Spirit quietly said, "No."

Deliberately, I handed the money over. The agent took it and said, "You have up until the fifteenth of June to change your mind. After that there is no refund." My mouth was dry as I smiled and said, "No problem!"

We were to sail to Canada by the end of June. I danced inside, pretending not to hear the Voice that said "No."

The next morning, as I stilled myself before the Lord, all that filled my mind was Canada and the tension caused by the Lord saying "No." There were no explanations, just "No." It was so real that I spent the whole hour arguing within myself.

For the next few mornings, I argued on. It was ridiculous. Everything was set for going; the money must have come from God, and Canada was waiting for what I had to say. But each day, the Voice within said, "No." I did not look forward to my day alone with God on the Donegal beach.

I decided to determine the will of God by the method commonly practiced among the Pentecostals: I put out a fleece. (The expression is taken from Judges and refers to Gideon's method of discovering God's will.) We had been having exceptionally wet weather that kept people from our meetings. I had a week of special meetings in a nearby village, so I used them as my fleece. "If the rain clears up and we have large crowds and at least one person is born again every night, I will take it as a sign that God wants me to go to Canada," I wrote solemnly in my journal.

I should have checked the weather forecast first. The rain cleared, the sun shone all week, and the meeting hall was packed. Many were born again at the end of each meeting. I was triumphant. Now I had proof that God wanted me to go!

In triumphant spirits, I drove further south the Monday after the meetings to Galway Bay. As I began meditation, the Voice within that had been silent for a week quietly said, "No." I was confused and began arguing. Everything had fit from the beginning, even the sign I had requested. My miserable inward dialogue went on all day, and I came home early. The days became dry. I meditated, but every page of Scripture seemed to say, "Do not go to Canada."

The fourteenth of June came, and I knew tomorrow was my last chance to change my mind. "Why should I?" I asked myself angrily as I drove to Market Hill. I would have to be crazy not to take such an opportunity, and I had obtained a leave of absence from the church.

All day on the fifteenth, I was conscious of deliberately refusing to listen to the Voice within. As I went to bed, I felt like saying stubbornly, "So there! I am going to Canada."

I did not meditate on the sixteenth or the seventeenth. The days dragged by as I became more miserable by the minute. On the twenty-second, a few days before sailing, I woke in the middle of the night. All was still, and I couldn't get back to sleep. Within me, the Voice was no longer still or small. *If you go to Canada, you go without the sense of My presence.*

So real was the experience that cold sweat broke on my forehead. I turned over, trying to pretend it hadn't happened. But as I lay on my side, the words seemed to be repeated in my spirit. I realized that the pillow was wet from my sweat. Jesus was alive, and at that moment, I wish He wasn't. I wished Christian meditation was a philosophy instead of fellowship with a real Person.

The words from Donegal Beach returned to me: *Be careful to do* — submission to the Lordship of Jesus. I was not merely someone who did not act as the world but listened and obeyed Jesus the living Word.

Lying through the night hours, I remembered the words of the Quaker. "In that silence, friend, much of your activity that you think is for God will drop away and be seen as useless. I suppose much work is *for* God-the trouble is it doesn't begin with God. In the silence of His presence all of life falls into place." I remembered begging him for the secret, asking him how one knew when to go and when to stay. His answer was as fresh as when he spoke it. "In the silence of light you know that this must go and that must be taken up. Life is lived *through* you, and it becomes a rest."

I knew what he was talking about now, but I wasn't too happy about it.

At 4:00 A.M., I slipped out of the house and walked into the fresh summer morning. I knew that God was the living God, and He had spoken to me. I knew what I had to do, but whimpered my reason, "The fifteenth was the last chance to change your mind; you're not going to lose a thousand dollars over this, are you?"

I knew that if I went to Canada, I would be silencing that presence who was the Lord of my life. To walk in obedience to that voice was worth more than a thousand dollars. I made my decision. I would lose the money and live with what people would say. I announced my decision to the family over breakfast, and they did not put up the argument I had expected.

On the way to Belfast, my heart began to sing. A glory filled the car, and joy began to well up that I had not known for weeks. "This is ridiculous," I laughed. "I am overjoyed at the thought of losing a thousand dollars."

I tried to explain to the Cunard agent that I was canceling the cabin because I could not go to Canada. "You won't understand this," I said nervously, "but I am a Christian, and I do not believe God wants me to go." She looked at me strangely and went to speak to her superiors. She came back smiling. There was a waiting list, and someone else would take my cabin. So, they decided to give me back my money. I mumbled thanks as she pushed the four hundred pounds across the counter. I was too stunned to say anything more.

It had been so long since I had enjoyed time alone that I took the following Saturday to visit Donegal. I anticipated the joy of walking alone with God. Apart from the joy of worship and renewing my desire to know God above all else, I wanted to understand what had happened.

After all, I questioned, everything was together, or it seemed to be, and the fleece — I decided not to pursue that, for I realized I had only been trying to make God say what I wanted Him to say. Then the thought occurred: *you knew what to do; you didn't need a fleece.*

That day, I sat in the sun and read through the Acts and the Epistles, seeking the nature of God's guidance. I concluded that since the Holy Spirit had come and joined Himself to the spirits of men, there was no guidance that appealed to the outward senses but only from walking in the light within. Colossians 3:15 put it together for me. *And let the peace of Christ rule in your hearts, to which indeed you were called in one body; and be thankful.*

I had a note in the margin of my Bible that pointed out that the Greek word for "rule" meant "to rule as an umpire." That is precisely what happened to me. As I moved, God, my peace within, had been the umpire, making me aware that I was wrong.

Reading through Acts, I noted that God did not continually tell the apostles what to do. His directive voice was rare, usually when their life was set in a certain direction. After that they did the obvious as they walked in union with God. They did not continually run to get wisdom, for wisdom walked His life in them.

Once Paul was commissioned by the Spirit and the church (Acts 13:1-3), he did not perpetually seek guidance. He walked in the path that lay ahead of him. Once directed to take the gospel to the pagans, he did not pray over every opportunity to find God's mind — he took every opportunity he could find to follow God's direction.

God spoke within them only when the most obvious was not the plan. This guidance was more in terms of what *not* to do than what to do.

The second missionary journey was only undertaken because Paul wanted to see how his recently established churches were maturing. He had no call this time; he was only doing what was on his heart to do. Having fulfilled that desire, they took the most obvious course — to Ephesus. Then God spoke. He told them they were not to go there. *But He didn't tell them what they had to do.* They turned around to make plans to take the next most obvious course, which was Bithynia. As they were about to do so, they had an inward check again.

There was only one course left to take —to Troas. After that, they had run out of the apparent courses to take, for they were facing the

Chapter 18

Mediterranean. At that point, God spoke by way of a dream and directed them to Macedonia.

A great relief stole over me as the sun began to sink in the west. I had been threatened by people who talked of God as if He was always chatting with them, giving them reams of directions daily; this was not the picture that emerged from Acts. These men walked *with* God and *in* God. The only directions given were in moments of crisis.

From the first thought of going to Canada, I realized that the Spirit within had checked me. I had gone through those miserable weeks because I wouldn't believe He was telling me not to go. I would know better in the future.

From that day, I walked by common sense that was exposed daily to me by the Word of God and the light and wisdom of the Holy Spirit. Anytime there was an area of life in which I did not know what to do, I made the best decision I could. If it were wrong, I would sense again that "No" within my spirit and would gratefully change my plans.

A few months later, I left the church in Armagh and moved to the suburbs of Belfast. I traveled throughout Ireland, conducting evangelistic crusades in churches, auditoriums, and tents, wherever I could get an audience.

An American evangelist preached in Belfast, and during the time he spent in the area, we became good friends. Before he left, he invited me to preach in the church where he was a member in Seattle, Washington. He urged me to speak at their 1964-65 New Year's convention.

I laughed. I had no money for the fare as I had just purchased the bungalow we were presently living in. Yet, even as I laughed, the idea of going to Seattle gave deep peace and assurance to my spirit. The assurance deepened as I waited on the Lord in the days that followed. I knew that in God's perfect timing, we would go to the United States and begin whatever my future held in Seattle.

Chapter 19

It was late December when our Air Canada 707 jet descended through the falling snow to land in Vancouver, British Columbia. We were fortunate to be able to land; the Pacific Northwest was in the middle of its worst blizzard in years. No more planes took off for days. We were bussed down to Seattle to be in time for the New Year's convention.

The convention was a success, and immediately afterward, we loaded up our newly-acquired station wagon and began traveling south, stopping at a different church each night, staying in some places for a few days, but always moving and preaching. In Los Angeles, we toured east and south across the desert, coming finally to Duluth, Minnesota, where we turned again for Seattle via the Canadian provinces.

During the thousands of miles covered in car and plane, I continued to wait on the Lord, reinforcing the lessons I had learned in the early years. I had to take silence where I could find it. I would often drive out of the town where our meetings were being held and pull over to a rest area under a grove of towering pines. At other times, long after everyone was asleep, I would sit under a California moon by a swimming pool and visit with God. While going through the desert, my place of silence was in the back of the wagon, parked on a side street in Las Vegas!

But something was wrong, very wrong. For all the spiritual growth and light happening in my personal life, my public ministry was withering and slowly dying — if it had ever been alive.

Since entering Bible school, I had considered preaching and conducting services as my work that had to be accomplished for God. Into that work, I poured my best talent, thinking and planning. Success for me was defined as the ability to gather the largest crowds, preach as persuasively as possible, and then press them with all urgency to decide to accept Christ as Savior. My entire meeting was geared to the final five minutes, where I would call people to register their decision by coming forward to the front of the auditorium.

For me, *that* was the ministry. I believed it was my responsibility to use any and every method to achieve that goal. After each service, I had the sense of presenting my results to God, feeling that I had achieved His purposes on earth in what I had done; this had been my understanding of the ministry since Bible school days. I had absorbed books that had expounded hundreds of tested ways to make that all-important invitation and ensure results for God. The fact that these methods were the same as those used to sell insurance, though couched in religious terms, did not bother me. I sincerely believed, at that time, that any method that brought people out of their seats to make a decision to accept Christ must be right.

When I arrived in the United States, I met men who had worked for years seeking goals similar to the ones I had set myself to achieve. There was one significant difference. These men had the methods of the great American corporations at their fingertips. They talked of the same goals, but on a scale I had never dreamed possible.

The simple one-roomed church buildings I had left behind in Europe were boy scout huts compared to the vast complexes I now saw. Any church I had pastored could be totally viewed by standing at the front door. I was now introduced to large buildings requiring guided tours to be fully seen and appreciated.

I had to know how to accomplish such great things for God. Eagerly, I attended every conference and seminar for pastors and church leaders that I could fit into my schedule. Sitting in such lectures, I was taught, along with hundreds of others, how to be a church administrator and a salesman for Jesus. We were taught how to have the largest church in the United States and given the ingredients that assured us of a place in the top ten American Sunday schools. I came away excited and dedicated to having the largest meetings of any evangelist.

But a spiritual dichotomy was beginning to tear me in two. On the one hand, I was waiting on the Lord, seeking to apply all He said to my personal life and attitudes. On the other hand, in my preaching and planning for public meetings, I was sweating as I ran a marathon, seeking to achieve greater crowds and more results so that I could please God. Inevitably, the two paths moved further away from each other. I was a person in disintegration.

In 1966, we returned to England to conduct missions for the Anglican church. We stayed on afterward, making our home in the center of England, and from there, I preached throughout the British Isles. In 1967, I took a preaching tour of Saskatchewan, Canada, and returned through New York City. I had a week of meetings at Salem Gospel Tabernacle in Brooklyn. They asked me to pastor the church at the close of the meetings. I accepted and began to make immediate plans to emigrate to the States.

We took over the pastorate of the church in July 1968. It was a ray of hope in a dark sky. In a settled pastorate, I believed I could achieve the success I had seen in the churches on the West Coast. Brooklyn would be my El Dorado, where all the conferences and ideas gleaned from successful men would finally pay off.

As the pastor of the church, I had some success. In a short while, the numbers swelled, but I was not satisfied. However appreciative the people were, I knew I was not imparting God's life to them. I was *talking about* that life but not *imparting* it.

There was no question that since the day I had started to preach, God had used me, and hundreds had been genuinely converted as they walked to the front of the auditorium. But I knew I was not imparting what I had enjoyed deep within my spirit.

Chapter 19

Like a robot, I went through the motions every Sunday. The people were happy with my biblical presentations, but we were all a valley of dry bones.

The hours of personal meditation became nothing more than a time to prepare sermons and plan programs. I knew I was dying inside, but I did not know how to be resurrected. The cause of the malady was a mystery to me, and where it would one day end was a faceless nightmare. But still, I churned out the meetings and plans, striving to build God's church in New York City.

The road to Stowmarket was a memory etched in the journals I had kept. Salt-stained notebooks, some still with a grain or two of sand in the bindings, filled with jottings made on the beaches of Donegal, were ghosts from another life.

By November 1970, I had come to the end of the road. I decided to resign and enter secular employment. I could handle being a private Christian, but I could no longer struggle, trying to achieve God's purposes on earth. With a heart of lead, I presented my letter of resignation. In a stupor, I accepted the church's gift of a vacation in the Virgin Islands.

For the first time in seventeen years, I was not in the ministry. I did not have to produce a successful church or series of meetings. It meant that, for the first time, I could step outside of what had been my life and look at it objectively. What happened on the sunbaked sands of St. Thomas could have happened anywhere. Once I was no longer involved in the rat race of grasping for the largest crowds and most results, I was open to hearing the commentary of the Holy Spirit on ministry.

The habit of years caused me to turn again to the Scriptures and meditate, casually making notes in a small notebook I had brought with me. God brought it together while meditating on the beach under a coconut palm. It was in the words I was reading from Matthew 16, "I will build my church." It came to me with crystal clarity. The voice of God as clear was as any time I had heard the inner Voice.

I had been working for God. I had taken all my human strength, power, talents, and resources and, with it all, tried to do what only God could. Following the flash of insight, I walked the rocky beaches of the island, the Word of God again speaking to me, giving me a new understanding of the ministry. I felt I had been given vast riches.

I realized I could no more *minister* the Christian life than *live* it. He who *lived* His life in me was the One who waited for me to let Him *minister* His life to others through my lips. It was no longer a matter of sweating at producing a word for God. I was free from that responsibility. My ministry was to be an act of worship, originating in God, flowing from Him through me, returning to its source, and giving Him the praise and glory. All my ministry had been something I gave *to* God. Now I saw that it was to be something that came *from* God.

I withdrew my resignation and returned to the church. The new perspective showed at once. I threw all my carefully hoarded plans and programs into the trash can and entered upon a period of spiritual readjustment unparalleled in my life.

Until then, my days as a pastor had been spent in planning and administration. Now, I was directed from the Spirit within to spend that time waiting on the Lord in worship. It was a period of waiting quite different from anything I had known before. It seemed as if I had never waited on God until now. From this new perspective, all the years that had gone before were but a promise of what I was not experiencing.

The experience was one of coming to *total* helplessness. I had known helplessness in living; now, I saw that I was also helpless to minister. There was no more dichotomy. I was an integrated person resting helplessly in God.

If all comes from God, all that I was left to do was praise and worship Him. One day, a river of praise surged through me, demanding a more adequate expression of praise than I could say in English or tongues. I found myself singing praise to God.

Meditation came alive again. It seemed that all the old lessons were retaught with the fresh touch of the Spirit on them — notebooks filled with insights, psalms and prayers. Waiting on the Lord became the vehicle of receiving my own spiritual sustenance and the source of my sermons. The messages I preached on Sunday began to flow in the energy of life, imparting resurrection to those who heard.

The period of intense waiting came to an end, but I would never be the same. From then on, in meditation, I heard God's inner voice teaching me *and* those to whom I ministered through Scripture. Doors began to open across the nation, and a whole new ministry of life opened up for me.

In 1973, thousands were to gather on a farm in Morgantown, Pennsylvania, and I was asked to share a series of Bible studies on meditation. I was hesitant, for all I had learned was within the framework of being a full-time student of the Bible. Could it be brought into the lives of people who worked daily at a secular job?

The response amazed me. It did not matter who the individual was. A new dynamic came into the Christian life when the principles were applied. Peace and creative joy flowed through the eager teens and Wall Street executives, not to mention housewives, as they set aside time to meditate and wait on the Lord. Pastors wrote about a new ministry emerging as they waited on the Lord. One Episcopal priest said that he danced around the room when he realized that the risen Jesus was speaking to him through the Bible by the Spirit.

Christian meditation is the most dynamic dimension that has ever been known. It is available to all whose eyes have been opened by the Spirit. It only takes the stilling of our busy souls to listen to Him, for He is ever waiting to fellowship with us beyond the silence.

Epilogue

It was April 1976. A light mist clung to the beach and across the mud flats of the River Thames. I walked briskly down the manicured cliffs from the old family home. At the bottom was the beach. The morning air was chilly, and I pulled my coat around me.

My preaching tour that had taken me across England was nearly over, and I had stopped off for two days to visit with my father and relatives. Now, in the quiet of the morning, I came to the beach to meditate.

The dry sand crunched beneath my feet. Through the mist, a gull cackled from a breakwater. Suddenly, my heart leaped, and my eyes brimmed. It was twenty-three years since I had walked this beach, driven by the call within my heart: *God wants to speak to you.*

I began walking out on the mud flats that stretched for over a mile at low tide. Mussel beds and cockle shells crunched under my feet. Nearly a mile from shore, alone in the mist, I raised my hands and began to sing praise to God. It was all of Him — He had saved me and drawn me through all my mistakes to fellowship with Himself. In retrospect, all I had contributed was to open inside ears and listen — and that only because He had called me.

Whatever the future held, I did not know, but I did know that I was not alone. In all those unborn hours, I would know the reality of fellowship with God within.

I picked up a rock, threw it into the river, and shouted, "Hallelujah!"

About the Author

Malcolm Smith was born in London, England, immediately before World War II. He came to a personal knowledge of the Lord Jesus in his early teens. He experienced the infilling of the Holy Spirit that changed his life forever. From the very beginning of his life in Christ, he was 'arrested' by 1 John 4, "God is Love." He not only has love — but IS LOVE! The Holy Spirit fueled a passion for knowing HIS love in its fullness.

Malcolm has pursued that desire for the past 70-plus years. He began teaching in his early teens and was pastor of churches in London and Ireland before coming to the U.S. in 1964. While pastoring a church in Brooklyn, N.Y., he encountered the Holy Spirit that plunged him into the emerging Charismatic movement that opened all denominations to his message. Since then, he has traveled worldwide, teaching believers who they are in Christ.

He presently lives in Bandera, Tx. with his wife, Cheryl, who brings with her many years of ministry experience in women's prisons, having served as women's staff chaplain of Harris County Jail from '92-2002. They conduct retreats and bible schools and minister to a weekly fellowship on Sunday mornings in Bandera on the ministry ranch.

He has hundreds of hours of teaching on CD and mp3 and hundreds of video hours on YouTube at Malcolm Smith webinars.

For further information, find us online at www.unconditionallove-fellowship.com.

Also by Malcolm Smith

Power of the Blood Covenant
This Son of Mine (expanded edition)
Toxic Love (revised edition)

LEGACY SOCIETY

The Spirit Gives Life was published by The Writer's Society a Grace & Trinitarian Publishing Company. It was published as part of our Legacy Society Publishing honoring authors who have devoted their lives to preaching the good news.

www.thewriterssociety.online

Made in United States
North Haven, CT
09 April 2025